Other Works of Interest from St. Augustine's Press

Charles E. Rice, *Contraception and Persecution*

Leszek Kolakowski, *Religion: If There Is No God . . .*

Christopher Bruell, *Aristotle as Teacher*

Rémi Brague, O*n the God of the Christians*
(and on one or two others)

Bruce Fingerhut, *A Passover Haggadah for Christians*

Aristotle, *Physics, or Natural Hearing*
(trans. Glen Coughlin)

Aristotle, *On Poetics*
(trans. Seth Benardete andMichael Davis)

Germain Grisez, *God? A Philosophical Preface to Faith*

Peter Geach, *God & the Soul*

Edward Feser, *The Last Superstition:*
A Refutation of the New Atheism

Peter Kreeft, *The Philosophy of Jesus*

Peter Kreeft, *Summa Philosophica*

C.S. Lewis & Don Giovanni Calabria, *The Latin Letters of*
C.S. Lewis

Fulvio Di Blasi, et al., *Ethics without God?*

Fulvio Di Blasi, et al., *Virtue's End*

Nicholas Capaldi and Theodore Roosevelt Malloch,
America's Spiritual Capital

Albert Camus, *Christian Metaphysics and Neoplatonism*
(trans. Ronald D. Srigley)

Ralph C. Hancock, *Calvin and the Foundations of*
Modern Politics

Francis H. Parker, *The Story of Western Philosophy*

ABORTING ARISTOTLE

ABORTING ARISTOTLE

Examining Fatal Fallacies
in the Abortion Debate

Dave Sterrett

ST. AUGUSTINE'S PRESS
South Bend, Indiana

Manufactured in the United States of America.

1 2 3 4 5 6   20 19 18 17 16 15

Library of Congress Cataloging in Publication Data
Sterrett, Dave.
Aborting Aristotle: examining the fatal fallacies in the abortion debate / Dave Sterrett.
pages cm
Includes bibliographical references and index.
ISBN 978-1-58731-003-4 (hardback: alk. paper)
1. Aristotle. 2. Abortion – Moral and ethical aspects.
I. Title.
HQ767.15.S745 2015
179.7'6 – dc23   2015005659

∞ The paper used in this publication meets the minimum requirements of the American National Standard for Information Sciences – Permanence of Paper for Printed Materials, ANSI Z39.48-1984.

ST. AUGUSTINE'S PRESS
www.staugustine.net

TABLE OF CONTENTS

Introduction

More than forty years have passed since the landmark decision Roe v. Wade, which legalized abortion in the United States. But the abortion debate continues to rage amongst ethicists and the influencers of society in politics, government and the arts. This book seeks to examine these essential differences philosophically and will investigate the naturalistic worldview about humanity that is frequently held by much of the scholarly defenders of abortion. There are some metaphysical or meta-ethical ideas (including law of non-contradiction, substance, transcendence, and intrinsic personhood) that were taught by Aristotle and the scholastics influenced by him that are frequently denied by defenders of abortion. These philosophical convictions influence their ethical stances on the abortion debate.

The ancients and scholastics were not aware of embryology like we are today. They believed ensoulment came later. Yet the ancients and medieval thinkers provided much contribution to philosophy. Today, many prominent intellectuals believe that life begins at the conception and fully agree about the empirical scientific information concerning the unborn human embryo. What scientists know about the embryo today is vastly superior to that of the ancients and scholastics. Yet ethicists frequently take diametrically opposed positions on "personhood" and the ethics of abortion. It is true that some marketing slogans by supporting groups or politicians for abortion choice may claim that the unborn embryo is simply "tissue," a "potential baby," or "part of the woman's body." However, most scholarly ethicists, including Peter Singer,[1] David Boonin,[2] Michael Tooley,[3] and Judith Jarvis Thomson,[4] who defend abortion choice, fully agree with the scientific conclusions of the embryologists concerning unborn children. Abortion defender Peter Singer of Princeton University wrote:

> Whether a being is a member of a given species is something that can be determined scientifically, by an examination of the nature of the chromosomes in the cells of the living organisms. In this sense there is no doubt that from the first moments of its existence an embryo conceived from human sperm and eggs is a human being.[5]

Singer also stated, "The human embryo, fetus and disabled child are members of 'Homo sapiens.'"[6] David Bonin in his book *A Defense of Abortion* (Cambridge) wrote:

---

1   Peter Singer is the Ira W. DeCamp Professor of Bioethics at Princeton University, and a Laureate Professor at the Centre for Applied Philosophy and Public Ethics at the University of Melbourne.
2   David Boonin is professor at University of Colorado.
3   Michael Tooley is a professor at the University of Colorado.
4   Judith Jarvis Thomson is professor emerita at MIT.
5   Peter Singer, *Writings on an Ethical Life* (New York: HarperCollins Publishers Inc., 2000), 127.
6   Singer, 127.

The fact that this relation obtains between a zygote and us is, of course, a function of the fact that a zygote is a living member of our species and the fact that it thus has the potential to develop into a human adult in a continuous, gradual manner.[7]

Abortion defender Michael Tooley of the University of Colorado disagrees with pro-life proponents for placing too much emphasis on the scientific fact of the child being human. He wrote:

[The] most important reason for not using the expression 'human being' in such a way that it either entails that something is a person, or that it has a right to life is this. One of the crucial questions involved in the issue of the morality of abortion is that of the moral significance of the purely *biological* facts, such as the foetus's belonging to a certain species.[8]

Judith Jarvis Thomson, professor emerita at MIT said:

I am inclined to think also that we shall probably have to agree that the fetus has already become a person well before birth. Indeed, it comes as a surprise when one first leans how early in its life it begins to acquire human characteristics. By the tenth week, for example, it

7   David Boonin, *A Defense of Abortion* (Cambridge: Cambridge University Press, 2003), 33.
8   Michael Tooley, *Abortion and Infanticide* (Oxford: Oxford University Press, 1983), 61.

already has a face, arms and legs, fingers and toes; it has internal organs, and brain activity is detectable.[9]

Most embryologists including Micheline M. Matthews-Roth[10] and Keith Moore[11] specifically say the unborn embryo is a distinct human being, a member of the homo sapiens species. Micheline M. Matthew-Roth, professor at Harvard Medical School, stated:

> We know from embryology that a new life begins with the formation of the zygote, the cell formed from the union of egg and sperm in fertilization – this is scientific fact, not religious doctrine.[12]

Within this commonality of beliefs about the empirical scientific data regarding the human embryo, it seems that

9   Judith Jarvis Thomson, *Rights, Restitution & Risk* (Cambridge: Harvard University Press, 1986), 1.
10   Micheline M. Matthews-Roth is professor at Harvard Medical School, retrieved at http://www.npr.org/programs/specials/stemcells/viewpoints.mathews.html).
11   "Human development begins after the union of male and female gametes or germ cells during a process known as *fertilization* (conception). Fertilization is a sequence of events that begins with the contact of a *sperm* (spermatozoon) with a *secondary oocyte* (ovum) and ends with the fusion of their *pronuclei* (the haploid nuclei of the sperm and ovum) and the mingling of their chromosomes to form a new cell. This fertilized ovum, known as a *zygote*, is a large diploid cell that is the beginning, or *primordium, of a human being.*" Keith Moore, *Essentials of Human Embryology* (Toronto: BC Decker Inc, 1988), 2. Keith Moore is professor emeritus, and former Chair of Anatomy at the University of Toronto, Ontario, Canada.
12   Micheline M. Matthews-Roth is professor at Harvard Medical School, retrieved at http://www.npr.org/programs/specials/stemcells/viewpoints.mathews.html).

many philosophers' ethical conclusions and differences concerning abortion are often rooted in several key underlying metaphysical or meta-ethical ideas about reality. We will closely examine those metaphysical distinctions. Rather than disputing the scientific evidence that scholars on both sides tend to agree, we will be able to show where the real disagreement lies in the abortion debate.

This book has eight related points that are critical to a defense of the intrinsic personhood of unborn children. It will argue for personhood as a reality that is united to one's nature rather than something that society determines. We will examine these key points that defenders of abortion often challenge or consider non-essential in the abortion debate.

There is a great tradition consisting of ancient and medieval philosophers who affirm immaterial realities. Plato, Aristotle, Augustine, Avicenna, Anselm, Duns Scotus and Thomas Aquinas are some of the most influential. Many contemporary ethicists who defend abortion rights have rejected or ignored many of the metaphysical notions of these classical and medieval philosophers. I will emphasize the philosopher Aristotle primarily as a key philosopher whose metaphysical ideas will be compared to key themes related to the abortion debate.

In the following chapters, I will frame the abortion debate with specific consideration to the *key metaphysical topics* that shape the ethical debate on abortion. First, I will provide a case for the reality of metaphysics and demonstrate that materialistic naturalism is not the best explanation of reality. Later, I will focus on particular metaphysical concepts including sanctity, substance and personhood that influence the ethical debate on abortion.

Chapter 1.

Aristotle and Thomas Jefferson

The great Greek philosopher Aristotle (384 BC–322 BC) and America's founding father, Thomas Jefferson, were alike in some respects. Both men were brilliant and influential. Aristotle was one of the sharpest Greek thinkers of his day, a writer on politics, science, education and philosophy. Aristotle was the tutor to Alexander the Great and well versed in all sorts of intellectual disciplines. Jefferson, likewise, was a brilliant statesman, an educator, an architect, a trained lawyer, and well versed in all sorts of science. Both Aristotle and Jefferson were passionately committed to truth and were among the most influential thinkers of their society.

Sometimes their teaching was false and sometimes they acted hypocritically with their own good teaching. Thomas Jefferson was one of the first statesmen in the world to articulate the evils of slavery. Henry Wiencek wrote:

> In his original draft of the Declaration, in soaring, damning, fiery prose, Jefferson denounced the slave trade as an "execrable commerce . . . this assemblage of horrors," a "cruel war against human nature itself, violating its most sacred rights of life & liberties."[1]

1   http://www.smithsonianmag.com/history/the-dark-side-of-thomas-jefferson-35976004/#poJqgRHhHDJ2zu1H.99.

In the 1770s, he wanted to abolish a practice that was almost universal. But Jefferson forsook his own teaching practically by indulging in the evils that he condemned.

Aristotle was brilliant in defending natural rights, virtue ethics, the laws of identity, and human dignity; but he was in favor of abortion, infanticide, and slavery. Aristotle and Jefferson did not agree with each other in all areas; yet, sadly, our society has thrown out the good that these men have provided us through their teachings. If we practiced what Jefferson wrote—"all men were created equal"—racism would be abolished. Sadly, instead of simply throwing out Jefferson's *hypocrisy* (owning slaves), a good number of America's educators and politicians have also thrown out Jefferson's notion of "law," his classical notion of "right to life," and his notion of an intelligent, transcendent "Creator." Likewise, the current educational and governmental leaders in the West have also thrown out Aristotle. Some of his science is out of date, and no doubt some of his beliefs about women and slavery are certainly morally wrong, but we have thrown out much of his good teaching about logic, philosophy and virtue.

Historian David Brion Davis wrote that "[Thomas Jefferson] was one of the first statesmen in any part of the world to advocate concrete measures for restricting and eradicating Negro slavery." In 1778, under Jefferson's leadership, the Virginia General Assembly banned the importing of slaves into Virginia. This was one of the original jurisdictions in the world to ban the slave trade, and all other states except South Carolina eventually followed. But in the 1790s Jefferson became silent on the issue of slavery. Madison Hemmings, the son of Sally Hemmings, said that his mother, one of Jefferson's slaves, became Jefferson's concubine when she was just a teenager and became pregnant by him in Paris in 1789. By being a slave owner, Jefferson acted hypocritically. He taught that "all men were created equal and endowed by their creator with certain unalienable rights: life, liberty and the pursuit of happiness." But in practice, Jefferson's life undermined his teaching. Peter Singer, one of the leading defenders of abortion said of Jefferson:

> Thomas Jefferson, who was responsible for writing the principle of the equality of men into the American Declaration of Independence, saw this point. It led him to oppose slavery even though he was unable to free himself fully from his slaveholding background. He wrote in a letter to the author of a book that emphasized the notable intellectual achievements of Negros in order to refute the then common view that they had limited intellectual capacities: "Be assured that no person living wishes more sincerely than I do, to see a complete refutation of the doubts I myself have entertained and expressed on the grade of understanding allotted to them by nature, and to find that they are on a par with ourselves . . . but whatever be their degree of talent it is no measure of their rights. Because Sir Isaac Newton was superior to others in understanding, he was not therefore lord of the property or person of others."[2]

Peter Singer (whom we will be critiquing at length) observed that although some of Jefferson's teaching was

2   Singer, *Writings on an Ethical Life*, 32.

hypocritical, some of it was good. On the other hand Singer rejects much of the metaphysics of Aristotle, but endorses Aristotle's defense of infanticide. Throughout this book, I will argue that Singer should have accepted Aristotle's metaphysics, but rejected Aristotle's agreement of infanticide. Singer said, "Both Plato and Aristotle recommended the killing of deformed infants." Singer says that it was Christianity that was responsible for the "change in Western attitudes since Roman times to infanticide" and gave us the "doctrine of the sanctity of human life." Peter Singer hopes the time has come for atheists to reassess the morality of infanticide "without assuming the Christian moral framework that has, for so long, prevented any fundamental reassessment."[3] It is true that Christianity was responsible for changing the Western attitudes about abortion. The early Christian book called the Didache stated:

> The second commandment of the teaching: You shall not murder. You shall not commit adultery. You shall not seduce boys. You shall not commit fornication. You shall not steal. You shall not practice magic. You shall not use potions. You shall not procure [an] abortion, nor destroy a newborn child. (*Didache* 2:1–2)

Tertullian,[4] one of the earliest church fathers, articulated a case against abortion. Robert H. Brom, Bishop of San Diego, wrote a tract that collected some of

3   Peter Singer, *Practical Ethics* (Cambridge, United Kingdom: Cambridge University Press, 1993), 173.
4   http://www.catholic.com/tracts/abortion.

Tertullian's teaching that we will consider. Tertullian said:

> In our case, a murder being once for all forbidden, we may not destroy even the fetus in the womb, while as yet the human being derives blood from the other parts of the body for its sustenance. To hinder a birth is merely a speedier man-killing; nor does it matter whether you take away a life that is born, or destroy one that is coming to birth. That *is* a man which is *going to be* one; you have the fruit already in its seed (*Apology* 9:8 [A.D. 197]).
>
> Among surgeons' tools there is a certain instrument, which is formed with a nicely-adjusted flexible frame for opening the uterus first of all and keeping it open; it is further furnished with an annular blade, by means of which the limbs [of the child] within the womb are dissected with anxious but unfaltering care; its last appendage being a blunted or covered hook, wherewith the entire fetus is extracted by a violent delivery.
>
> There is also [another instrument in the shape of] a copper needle or spike, by which the actual death is managed in this furtive robbery of life: They give it, from its infanticide function, the name of *embruosphaktes*, [meaning] "the slayer of the infant," which of course was alive. . . .
>
> [The doctors who performed abortions] all knew well enough that a living being had been conceived, and [they] pitied this most luckless infant state, which had first to be put to death,

to escape being tortured alive (*The Soul*, 25 [A.D. 210]).

Now we allow that life begins with conception because we contend that the soul also begins from conception; life taking its commencement at the same moment and place that the soul does (ibid., 27).

The law of Moses, indeed, punishes with due penalties the man who shall cause abortion [Ex. 21:22–24] (ibid., 37).

What we learn from Tertullian is that Christianity was against abortion and contrary to the teachings of society. We also learn that abortion is nothing new. Even though today abortionists have more sophistication with their suction instruments and sonograms, some of the procedures are similar to those of the ancient world. Dr. Anthony Levatino, who specializes in Obstetrics and Gynecology, completed 1,200 abortions before becoming pro-life and ceasing to perform abortions. On May 23, 2013, he spoke before members of a congressional committee and described performing a second trimester Dilation and Evacuation (D&E):

. . . The toughest part of a D&E abortion is extracting the baby's head. The head of a baby that age is about the size of a large plum and is now free floating inside the uterine cavity. You can be pretty sure you have hold of it if the Sopher clamp is spread about as far as your fingers will allow. You will know you have it right when you crush down on the clamp and see white gelatinous material coming through the cervix. That was the baby's brains. You can then extract the skull pieces. Many times a little face will come out and stare back at you.[5]

Levatino added, "These procedures are brutal by nature." Tertullian, who lived in the ancient world, also knew that abortion practices are brutal. Christians wanted to put a stop to it.

Christianity's position on abortion is contrary to Aristotle's defense of abortion, but not contrary to Aristotle's logic and metaphysics. Does Aristotle's bad teaching about abortion mean that we should get rid of all Aristotle's teaching? I will argue that today's defenders of abortion have thrown out the good with the bad. Aristotle, like Jefferson, provides much good teaching about natural rights and human dignity, and notions like virtue and equality, but we have thrown out the baby with the bathwater. In *Aborting Aristotle*, I will defend some of the good that Aristotle taught, such as the laws of logic and metaphysics. A restoration of Aristotle's philosophy, alongside contemporary embryology, and the acknowledgement of humans being dependent on the existence of the Creator, will help to shape individuals' minds concerning the unborn.

5   Dr. Anthony Levatino. *H.R.1797 – Pain-Capable Unborn Child Protection Act*, sponsored Rep. Frank Trents, Congress.gov/ https://beta.congress.gov/bill/113th-congress/house-bill/1797, accessed on May 23, 2013.1   Aristotle, *Physics*, 184a10–21.

Chapter 2.

Metaphysics Is Essential to the Ethical Debate on Abortion

Metaphysics has been defined as the branch of philosophy that deals with the first principles of things. In Aristotle's philosophical writings, he stated that he was examining "first principles" or origins (from the Greek term, *archai*). Aristotle said:

> In every systematic inquiry (*methodos*) where there are first principles, or causes, or elements, knowledge and science result from acquiring knowledge of these; for we think we know something just in case we acquire knowledge of the primary causes, the primary first principles, all the way to the elements. It is clear, then, that in the science of nature as elsewhere, we should try first to determine questions about the first principles. The naturally proper direction of our road is from things better known and clearer to us, to things that are clearer and better known by nature; for the things known to us are not the same as the things known unconditionally (*hap-lôs*). Hence it is necessary for us to progress, following this procedure, from the things that are less clear by nature, but clearer to us, towards

things that are clearer and better known by nature.[1]

Metaphysics also applies to concepts such as being, knowing, substance, cause, identity, time, and space. However, to be clear and to avoid any hasty generalizations, we will *not* argue that all scholarly proponents of abortion necessarily reject or consistently deny all the points that will be mentioned. Yet, the reason this book will focus on these classical *metaphysical or meta-ethical themes* is that some ethicists simply believe that one can bypass certain metaphysical or meta-ethical concepts regarding humanity and dive right into the ethical discussion. For example, many contemporary defenders of abortion choice continue to follow Judith Jarvis Thomson in her 1971 violin analogy, in which she argued that the metaphysical nature (or personhood) of the unborn baby is not the key factor in deciding the moral permissiveness of abortion.[2] Thomson wrote, "I propose, then that we grant that the fetus is a person from the moment of conception."[3] Analogies and arguments that imply that the metaphysical nature is not primarily essential in the abortion debate will be examined and challenged in this book.

Most ethicists affirm that "persons" are beings to whom the values of "dignity," "rights," and "protection" apply. Although most ethicists agree that "personhood" is important, they debate whether personhood is something intrinsic, united with the nature of that being, or something extrinsic that society determines based on

2   Judith Jarvis Thomson, *Rights, Restitution & Risk* (Cambridge: Harvard University Press, 1986), 1.
3   Ibid.

particular functions that a being can perform. The former say that a person is a person because of the type of being they are, i.e. humans. Therefore, many ethicists who oppose the killing of infants, do so because they believe that the unborn, like newborns and the mentally handicapped, still have intrinsic value based upon their nature, even though they cannot perform certain functions. On the other hand, some abortion choice advocates argue in defense of the killing of infants, mentally handicapped and elderly humans, because they believe that these humans do not achieve levels of consciousness, feel pain or perform certain functions. The abortion choice defenders conclude that these humans lose their privileges of personhood because personhood is a status based on levels of function or rights that are granted by society.

Augustine (354–430) taught that human beings were *intrinsically* valuable because they were *human*, not merely externally valuable for what they performed or the state recognized. During Augustine's day, Rome believed that the government was the one who decided personhood. As Richard Frothingham summarized, "The individual was regarded as of value only if he was part of the political fabric and able to contribute to its uses, as though it were the end of his being to aggrandize the State."[4] Boethius (480–524) believed that all human beings were persons, because they were human. He said that persons were individuals of a rational nature. And when Boethius refers to concepts like individuality and nature, he is agreeing with some of Aristotle's teaching on

4   Frothingham, R., *The Rise of the Republic of the United States* (Boston: Brown, 1910), 6.

metaphysics. To defend the personhood of the unborn, we will see how much of Aristotle's teaching is still relevant.

Recently, metaphysics has been under attack by some scholars in higher academia. This attack from some scientific materialists has influenced contemporary ethicists. More generally, some naturalists have implied that because of the advancements in physics all branches of philosophy are irrelevant in wrestling with questions concerning nature, origin and purpose. The award-winning physicist, Stephen Hawking, boldly pronounced in his chapter entitled, "The Mystery of Being" that "philosophy is dead."[5]

So why is *metaphysics* so important when addressing an issue like abortion? I am not using the term metaphysics to refer to the pseudo-Eastern, pantheistic, positive-thinking section of books about pop culture that attempt to blend Buddhism, Christianity and occultism. I am using the term Metaphysics (literally "after the Physics") following the major treatise of Aristotle (384 BC–322 BC).[6] Aristotle referred to metaphysics as "first philosophy," or "the study of being qua being." In *Metaphysics*, Aristotle examined not just particular physical things which are examined in physics, but also sought knowledge of causes, principles and natures. Metaphysics in general addresses questions that transcend physical particulars and asks questions like: Is there cause and effect? Is there such a thing as human nature? Do humans have rights? Are numbers real? Is there a soul? Are there

---

5   Stephen Hawking and Leonard Mlodinow, *The Grand Design* (New York: Random House, 2010), 5.
6   "Aristotle" retrieved on http://plato.stanford.edu/entries/aristotle/.

first principles and universals? Is reality both physical and non-physical? Does God exist?

Some of the Greek philosophers even believed that one could have knowledge of God in a non-religious way. Aristotle wrote, "The first mover, then, exists of necessity; and in so far as it exists by necessity, its mode of being is good, and it is in this sense a first principle."[7] He continued, "On such a principle, then, depend the heavens and the world of nature."[8] Aristotle, who wasn't as religious as his predecessors Socrates and Plato, believed that intellectually, this being existed. He said, "We say therefore that God is a living being, eternal, most good, so that life and duration continuous and eternal belong to God; for this is God."[9]

Metaphysics may also investigate "why" questions regarding the *telos* or purpose of nature. These are the subjects that transcend the empirical repeatable scientific method inside a laboratory and are investigated philosophically and logically.

Because metaphysics deals with that which is (and not what rocks dream about), a person's beliefs about any of these metaphysical questions just mentioned can influence one's ethical discussion. For example,[10] let us suppose that you have your back turned to your children, and you hear one of them cry out and ask you, "Can I kill this?" Before you answer that question, it is very

---

7 Aristotle, *Metaphysics*, XII.7.
8 Ibid.
9 Ibid.
10 I heard this example given by Scott Klusendorf, who gave summer lectures at Summit Ministries, Manitou Springs, Colorado during the summer of 2012. His website is http://www. prolifetraining.com/.

important to know what "this" actually is. Before you answer as a parent you will obviously want to turn around and see if your child is holding a mosquito or his younger brother. Most parents have practical knowledge that it is morally permissible for your child to kill the mosquito but certainly not another human being. If humans are merely physical material cells and there exist no transcendent realities or objective moral laws, then it is much more difficult to argue that an act like abortion is objectively, morally wrong. However, if concepts like dignity, personhood, soul, and other transcendent realities really do exist amongst unborn humans, then there are good reasons to argue that abortion is truly wrong.

In the history of Western philosophy, many philosophers have been influenced by Plato or by Aristotle. According to Alfred North Whitehead, "The safest general characterization of the European philosophical tradition is that it consists of a series of footnotes to Plato."[11] The three great Greek philosophers — Socrates, Plato, and Aristotle — spoke of immaterial realities and transcendence. To give a very brief historical summary: Plato argued that the physical world and sense experience did not provide true knowledge, but only opinion and belief. The minute one says that the fire is hot, it has died out. One may think he sees a perfect rectangle, but only by thinking mathematically about geometry can one understand "rectangle-ness" in one's mind. One person in the room may feel warm, while another person may feel hot. Our senses tell us certain things about the universe, but we discover that our senses often deceive us. Plato argued that the physical

---

11   Alfred North Whitehead, *Process and Reality* (New York: Free Press, 1979), 39.

world is like shadows in a cave, images and reflections of the true reality. He believed that the true reality itself consists of transcendent forms of humanness, mathematical realities and the higher forms of justice, love and the idea of the good. Plato was a metaphysical dualist who affirmed that the immaterial world was unchanging, eternal, and objectively true, while the physical world was a shadow.

In contrast, Aristotle, Plato's student, dismissed Plato's dualism. As an empiricist, Aristotle emphasized and observed the physical world while making categorizations. Yet Aristotle affirmed the immaterial and sought universals and discovery of natures. William Lawhead summarized how these two great philosophers differ:

> Having dismissed Plato's extreme dualism, where does Aristotle locate the forms? To answer this question, he turns to the only reality we have — the natural world around us. For Plato's picture of transcendent Forms, Aristotle substitutes the notion of immanent forms. The forms can only be the cause and explanation of things if they are an intrinsic part of things. There is no abstract Form of "Tableness" apart from this world. There are only individual tables, each exhibiting the form that identifies something as a table.[12]

Aristotle's intrinsic notion of forms as the immanent form of something like person has implications for ethics. Edward Feser said, "Abandoning Aristotelianism, as the

---

12 William F. Lawhead, *The Voyage of Discovery* (Belmont: Wadsworth/Thomson, 2002), 76.

founders of modern philosophy did, was the single greatest mistake ever made in the entire history of Western Thought."[13] Influenced by Aristotle, Thomas Aquinas wrote, "A small error in the beginning of something is a great one in the end."[14] Some intellectuals will consciously make a philosophical commitment by denying realities such as meaning, nature, God, dignity, and natural law. Some might make the decision based on rational convictions while many others deny or ignore some philosophical truths for personal motives. Aldous Huxley wrote:

> I had motives for not wanting the world to have a meaning; consequently assumed that it had not; and was able without any difficulty to find satisfying reasons for this assumption. The philosopher who finds no meaning for this world is not concerned exclusively with the problem of pure metaphysics; he is also concerned to prove that there is no valid reason why he personally should not do as he wants to. . . . For myself . . . the philosophy of meaninglessness was essentially an instrument of liberation, sexual and political.[15]

Huxley acknowledges a connection between meaning and metaphysics, but also admits personal reasons for

---

13 Edward Feser, *The Last Superstition* (South Bend: St. Augustine's Press, 2008), 51.

14 St. Thomas Aquinas *On Being and Essence,* quoted by Edward Feser, *The Last Superstition* (South Bend: St. Augustine's Press, 2008), vii.

15 Aldous Huxley, *End and Means* (New York: Garland Publishers, 1938), 270–73.

wanting a philosophy without meaning that would justify the freedom of his sexual and political ideas. Some ethicists and medical professionals choose not to think seriously about major metaphysical and epistemological ideas. Some may be less intentional, perhaps being busy pursuing a career or the pragmatics of their career, while unconsciously picking up the ideas of culture or their academic community without analyzing why they believe those ideas to be true. Then a politician or even a Supreme Court justice uses those ideas to deny the nature of an unborn human person, thereby falsely persuading the masses that it is morally good and liberating for women to abort their own babies. These philosophical ideas frequently harm children, their parents, the elderly and society. Plato wrote in *Phaedrus*:

> And when the orator instead of putting an ass in the place of a horse puts good for evil being himself as ignorant of their true nature as the city on which he imposes is ignorant; and having studied the notions of the multitudes, falsely persuades them not about "the shadow of an ass," which he confounds with a horse but about good which he confounds with evil — what will be the harvest which rhetoric will be likely to gather after the sowing of that seed?[16]

Many contemporary orators of society are convinced that Aristotle's philosophy of the law of non-contradiction,

16 Plato, *Phaedrus* 260C, cited by Edward Feser, *The Last Superstition*, (South Bend, St. Augustine's Press, 2008), vii.

ontological existence, substance, and human rights are irrelevant or unknowable. The ethical beliefs of society's influencers have molded many people's beliefs about abortion and human dignity, whether society realizes it or not.

Chapter 3.

Denying the Metaphysics
of Persons Is Self-Refuting

I mentioned that physicist Stephen Hawking declared in his chapter entitled, "The Mystery of Being," that "philosophy is dead."[1] Some students of philosophy might read a statement like that and then reply, "Is that *his* philosophy?" Why? Because Hawking has not provided empirically demonstrated scientific proof, but rather has made a philosophical assertion about the mystery of being. His book not only provides scientific theory but also repeats some of the major philosophical assertions and questions about reality. He wrote,

> Although we are puny and insignificant on the scale of the cosmos, this makes us in a sense the lords of creation. To understand the universe at the deepest level, we need to know not only how the universe behaves, but why. Why is there something rather than nothing? Why do we exist?[2]

Although some abortion-choice advocates are philosophical materialists or naturalists who favor moral

1   Stephen Hawking and Leonard Mlodinow, *The Grand Design* (New York: Random House, 2010), 5.
2   Ibid., 13.

relativism, others would argue against relativism; some would go as far to follow Thomson and argue for objectivity, while accepting some notions of Aristotle's ethics.[3] However, when an ethicist like Paul Simmons who affirms moral objectivity also downplays metaphysics, he has made assertions that are self-refuting in nature. Norman Geisler defined self-refuting statements as "those which fail to satisfy their own criteria of validity or acceptability."[4] Obvious examples of self-refuting statements might include: "I cannot type a word of English," "All words are meaningless," or "The truth about reality is unknowable." These statements have implications that violate Aristotle's definition of truth and the law of non-contradiction. The law of non-contradiction says P cannot be both P and non-P at the same time and in the same sense. The person who has made a profession that he cannot speak a word of English, has spoken in English while at the same time claiming that one cannot speak in English. Likewise, the person who has claimed that the truth about reality is unknowable is implying that he has some *knowledge* about reality, namely that he *knows* it is unknowable, while at the same time claiming that knowledge is unknowable. Some ethicists claim a lack of knowledge concerning the embryo, but will frequently then claim knowledge of what we ethically ought to do with embryos.

Aristotle sets forth a very clear correspondence view of truth. The correspondence view says that there should

3   Gilbert Harman and Judith Thomson, *Moral Relativism and Moral Objectivity* (Oxford: Wiley-Blackwell,1996)
4   Norman Geisler, *Baker Encyclopedia of Christian Apologetics* (Grand Rapids: Baker, 1999), 703.

be an identity between two things for truth to exist. Aristotle writes, "To say of what is that it is not, or what is not that it is, is false, while to say of what is that it is, and of what is not that it is not, is true." Aristotle also includes an extremely simple formulation of the correspondence theory of truth. This theory is tied to the law of non-contradiction. The key that ties these two together is the word "is." Non-contradiction says "is" and "is-not" are opposite. Correspondence rests upon a relevant sameness in the proposition and the state of affairs. When one uses the word "is" in the predication, "The ball is red," he is making a statement of predication. When he makes the assertion of existence, "Atoms are" he is asserting existence. These statements assume the law of non-contradiction and correspondence theory to be true. This very fact is fatal to all non-correspondence theories of truth as they rely on the correspondence theory to make their case (note how they use the word "is" in saying that truth *is* their theory, pragmatism, coherence, etc.). So in critiquing the popular notion of relativism that some attribute to Heraclitus, Aristotle says, "ἀδύνατον γὰρ ὁντινοῦν ταὐτὸν ὑπολαμβάνειν εἶναι καὶμὴ εἶναι, καθάπερ τινὲς οἴονται λέγειν Ἡράκλειτον."[5] ("For it is impossible for someone to 'take up' the same thing to be and not to be, according to what some believe Heraclitus said.") The Greek verb that Aristotle is using is εἶναι, the present, active, infinitive form of εἰμί which simply means "is" or "existence" or "I am."

Aristotle's principle of non-contradiction applies three ways:

1. Ontological: "It is impossible for the same attribute at

5   Aristotle, *Metaphysics.* 4.1005b

once to belong and not to belong to the same thing and in the same relation" (*Metaphysics* 1005B19-20).

2. Psychological: "then clearly it is impossible for the same man to suppose at the same time that the same thing is and is not" (*Metaphysics* 1005B23-24).

3. Logical: "The most certain of all basic principles is that contradictory propositions are not true simultaneously" (*Metaphysics* 1011B13-14).[6]

Also classically, Plato in the *Theaetus* provides an example of Protagoras implying a violation of the law of non-contradiction, contained in a self-refuting statement in a conversation between Socrates and the mathematician Theodorus:

> Socrates: Protagoras, for his part, admitting as he does that everyone's opinion is true, must acknowledge the truth of his opponents' belief about his own belief, where they think he is wrong.
>
> Theodorus: Certainly.
>
> Socrates: That is to say, he would acknowledge his own belief to be false, if he admits that the belief of those who think him wrong is true?
>
> Theodorus: Necessarily.[7]

Here is a specific example how the discussion of meta-

---

6   Jan Łukasiewicz, "On the Principle of Contradiction in Aristotle", *Review of Metaphysics* 24 (1971): 485–509. Łukasiewicz described the ontological, psychological, and logical distinction by Aristotle.

7   Plato, *Theaetetus* 171.A.B. cited by William F. Lawhead, *The Voyage of Discovery* (Belmont: Wadsworth/Thomson, 2002), 46.

physics is related to the issue of the ethics of abortion. Paul Simmons, who is a clinical professor of medical ethics at the University of Louisville, wrote an article for Oxford's *Journal of Church and State*, arguing that metaphysics is based solely on religious speculation. Aristotle's law of non-contradiction could apply to this idea of his. If all metaphysics is based upon religious speculation then *is this metaphysical statement by Dr. Simmons based upon religious speculation?*

Philosopher Francis Beckwith responded to Paul Simmons and said, "*All positions* on abortion presuppose some metaphysical point of view, and for this reason, the abortion-choice position Simmons defends is not entitled to a privileged philosophical standing in our legal framework."[8] Beckwith says of Simmons, "He then cites, as an example of what is not speculative metaphysics, the *viability standard* proposed by the Court in Roe."[9] Simmons attacks concepts like personhood and lumps it with the metaphysics of religious groups. Consider these claims by Simmons regarding metaphysics:

> Of special concern are those proposals regarding fetal personhood that rest on abstract metaphysical opinion, and the actions of various religious groups whose determination to shape policy results in actions which infringe upon the religious liberties of others."[10]

8 Francis Beckwith, *Defending Life* (Cambridge: Cambridge University Press, 2007), 44.
9 Ibid.
10 Paul D. Simmons, "Religious Liberty and Abortion Policy: Casey as 'Catch 22'" *Journal of Church and State* 42.1 (Winter 2000): 69–88.

We could apply a self-refuting test and ask him, "Is this special concern of yours infringing upon others who might disagree with your metaphysical opinion?" Simmons has not provided empirical data that has refuted metaphysics; rather he made a metaphysical assertion. Again, Simmons said:

> The first principle of religious liberty is that laws will not be based upon abstract metaphysical speculation, but will be fashioned through democratic processes in which every perspective is subject to critical analysis.[11]

Perhaps I could ask Simmons, "What do you mean by first principle of religious liberty? Is that principle physical or metaphysical? Is it universal or just relative to your interpretation of religious liberty?" Again, throughout Simmons' article, he makes references that include metaphysical concepts such as, "The abortion debate has furthered the awareness that both the personhood of women and their exercise of procreative rights are uniquely at stake in pregnancy."[12] This statement that includes the words "personhood" and "rights" comes immediately after attacking the arguments used by religious people who believe in the personhood of the embryo in his section entitled, "Rejecting Abstract Metaphysics as Law."[13] In addition, Simmons wrote, "the woman is the final arbiter in the abortion decision"[14] because men "do

11 Ibid.
12 Ibid.
13 Ibid.
14 Ibid.

not know personally or experientially the threat and burden of an unwanted pregnancy."[15] Again, we could apply a self-contradictory principle to Simmons and then ask, "Why is he, as a man, who does not know pregnancy personally or experientially, able to be an 'arbiter' on the abortion debate for anyone who disagrees with his view of abortion rights?" Also, if Simmons is correct that men should not have the "final say" or be the "arbiter" then has he invalidated Roe v. Wade, the landmark decision on abortion, because it was decided by *seven men* (7-2) on the Supreme Court in 1973.

15   Ibid.

Chapter 4.

Lacking Epistemological Preciseness Concerning Human Beings Does Not Disprove the Truth about Their Ontological Existence

In the last section, we discussed how ethicist Paul Simmons spoke very unfavorably about metaphysics. Some ethicists who favor abortion choice are more subtle when they downplay classical notions of metaphysics concerning reality. One of the more subtle ways is to argue that because some humans may lack precise *knowledge* concerning certain specifics about fertilization or when the child experiences pain, the *metaphysical or ontological reality* must not exist. The one who argues this seems to be confusing epistemology (the study of knowledge) with ontology (metaphysics or the nature of being). One of the most scholarly philosophical defenses of abortion in recent years is *A Defense of Abortion* by David Boonin, published by Cambridge University Press. The preface of Boonin's book is emotionally gripping for readers on either side of the debate as he stated:

> The other reason that this book was difficult to write is more personal. On the desk in my office where most of this book was written and revised, there are several pictures of my son, Eli. In one, he is gleefully dancing on the sand along the Gulf of Mexico, the cool ocean breeze

wreaking havoc with his wispy hair. In a second, he is tentatively seated in the grass in his grandparents' backyard, still working to master the feat of sitting up on his own. In a third, he is only a few weeks old, clinging firmly to the arms that are holding him and still wearing the tiny hat for preserving body heat that he wore home from the hospital. Through all of the remarkable changes that these pictures preserve, he remains unmistakably the same little boy.

In the top drawer of my desk, I keep another picture of Eli. This picture was taken on September 7, 1993, 24 weeks before he was born. The sonogram image is murky, but it reveals clearly enough a small head tilted back slightly, and an arm raised up and bent, with the hand pointing back toward the face and the thumb extended out toward the mouth. There is no doubt in my mind that this picture, too, shows the same little boy at a very early stage in his physical development. And there is no question that the position I defend in this book entails that it would have been morally permissible to end his life at this point.

Perhaps it will be thought distasteful of me to mention this fact. I find, on the contrary, that what is distasteful is to think of abortion as a purely theoretical issue, an intriguing philosophical problem that should be grappled with only in abstract and impersonal terms.[1]

---

1   David Boonin, *A Defense of Abortion* (Cambridge: Cambridge University Press, 2003), xiii.

Now, in this opening, Boonin is affirming his *knowledge* that the sonogram is showing the same little boy, his son Eli. Later Boonin *affirms* continuity but rejects its right to life. He asks, "So why should the fact of continuity between the zygote and us be taken as support for the conclusion that if we have right to life, then so does a zygote?"[2] Boonin later adds, "For if the relation of continuity forces us to continually push the point at which we have an individual with a right to life back further and further, then why should it stop at the moment of conception? Why not take it that the sperm and the egg must also be thought of as having this right?"[3] Boonin then seeks to respond to the defender of the embryo who says, "The only radically discontinuous event in the development history of an individual like you and me is the forming of the zygote at the moment of conception."[4] Boonin says that using the phrase "moment" of conception is misleading because some embryologist wrote that fertilization is itself a gradual process that typically takes about twenty-two hours from beginning to end.[5] He also says that we cannot draw the line precisely at brain activity because the precise timing of viability is unknown. In his footnote, Boonin provides further explanation:

> Relatedly, there is a sense in which we can draw a precise line with respect to these other criteria. Given our current state of knowledge about the relationship between brain states and mental

2   Ibid., 33.
3   Ibid., 35–36.
4   Ibid., 36.
5   Ibid., 37.

states, for example, we cannot *know* precisely when a fetus first has a certain kind of mental state or first has a certain kind of capacity, but we can still confidently say that there must be *some* specific moment when it first has them.[6]

Boonin's last statement shows that he is aware of the ontological reality of mental states coming to existence. However, he is also arguing that because of disagreement and lack of knowledge, the dignity of the human embryo is non-existent and abortion should still be justifiable. Boonin is not directly attacking metaphysics or the ontological nature the same way as did Simmons, whom we previously addressed. To use Boonin's own words, he is arguing that "we *cannot know* precisely." The agnostic nature itself seems dogmatic rather than subjective.

Rather than saying, "I do not know precisely, because some scientists disagree," or "We do not know *right now*," Boonin seems to be claiming *knowledge* for all scientists, all philosophers, and all readers when he writes, "we *cannot* know precisely." While honest uncertainty should leave Boonin at agnosticism concerning what ought to be done, he and other ethicists often conclude with moral dogmatism, assuming that this lack of precise knowledge leads to the moral permissibility of abortion. Lack of moral knowledge does not indicate moral neutrality. Francis Beckwith provides this response to David Boonin:

> Boonin's raising of this important epistemological question (When do we know X is an individual organism and its germ cell progenitors

6   Ibid.

cease to be?) does not detract from the claim that a complete and living zygote is a whole human organism. It *may be* that one cannot, with confidence, pick out the precise point at which a new being comes into existence between the time at which the sperm initially penetrates the ovum and a complete and living zygote is present. But how does it follow from that acknowledgement of agnosticism that one cannot say that zygote X is a human being? It seems to me that Boonin commits the fallacy of the beard: just because I cannot tell you when the stubble ends and a beard begins does not mean that I cannot distinguished bearded faces from clean-shaven ones. After all, abortion choice supporters typically pick out what they consider value-making properties — for example, rationality, having a self-concept, sentience, or organized cortical brain activity (as in the case of Boonin) — that they maintain justify one concluding that a being lacking one or all of them does not have a right to life. But it is nearly impossible to pick out at what precise point in a being's existence it acquires the correct trait, for example, when it becomes rational enough or has a sufficient amount of organized cortical brain activity to warrant a right to life. But it is doubtful whether the abortion-choice advocate would abandon her position on those grounds.[7]

7 Francis Beckwith, *Defending Life* (Cambridge: Cambridge University Press, 2007), 67.

Although in one instance those in favor of abortion choice agree with embryologists concerning the scientific fact of an embryo being a distinct human person, they then appeal to aspects of lacking a precise knowledge during the process of fertilization. However a major difference between pro-life advocates and those in favor of abortion choice is the ethical human life principle: "If in doubt, err on the side of human life." To give an analogy, let's suppose you are hunting with several friends and you see something moving behind a bush, but you are not sure if it's a deer or a person. You should refrain from shooting.

Lacking precise knowledge does not mean that one should assume that the unborn babies are not people. Robert Spitzer correctly observes, "The 'reasoning' of the majority of the Court in Roe v. Wade was grounded in a gratuitous and destructive assumption: when in doubt, *assume* that human life does not exists, and *assume*, as a consequence, that the killing of such life can be sanctioned."[8] This was the majority's reasoning in Roe v. Wade:

> Texas urges that, apart from the Fourteenth Amendment, life begins at conception and is present throughout pregnancy, and that, therefore, the State has a compelling interest in protecting that life from and after conception. We need not resolve the difficult question of when life begins. When those trained in the respective disciplines of medicine, philosophy, and theology are unable to arrive at any consensus, the

8   Robert J. Spitzer, *Ten Universal Principles* (San Francisco: Ignatius Press: 2011), 23.

judiciary, at this point in the development of man's knowledge, is not in a position to speculate as to the answer.[9]

In 1973, when the Justices of the Supreme Court answered, "The judiciary, at this point in the development of man's knowledge, is not in a position to speculate as to the answer,"[10] they did not defer their decision but rather used their position to rush their authoritative answer which would be imposed on the lives of over 57,000,000 unborn babies.

The philosophical idea of "I don't know exactly when life begins, therefore abortion is certainly morally permissible," was put into law by the Supreme Court in 1973 and intellectually defended by David Boonin in 2003. It has been employed in a similar fashion in the political arena. Earlier, I claimed that people who are not professional philosophers (such as politicians and poets) often make ethical applications based on philosophical ideas.

9   Roe v. Wade, 410 U.S. 113 (1973), Sec. IX. B cited in Robert J. Spitzer, Ten Universal Principles (San Francisco: Ignatius Press: 2011), 23.
10   Roe v. Wade, 410 U.S. 113 (1973), Sec. IX. B.

Chapter 5.

Naturalistic Materialism Is Not the Best Explanation for Reality

Many proponents of abortion choice who reject metaphysics hold a naturalistic philosophy generally about reality, and specifically about homo sapiens. I believe there are good reasons why naturalistic materialism, which is frequently assumed or believed by proponents of abortion, is not the best explanation for reality. Since there are some overlaps and disagreements concerning definitions of the words naturalism, materialism, and physicalism, I will attempt to describe what I mean by "naturalistic materialism." David Papineau in the *Stanford Encyclopedia of Philosophy* wrote:

> The term "naturalism" has no very precise meaning in contemporary philosophy. Its current usage derives from debates in America in the first half of the last century. The self-proclaimed "naturalists" from that period included John Dewey, Ernest Nagel, Sidney Hook and Roy Wood Sellars.[1]

1   David Papineau, "Naturalism," *The Stanford Encyclopedia of Philosophy* (Spring 2009 Edition), retrieved at <http://plato.stanford.edu/archives/spr2009/entries/naturalism/>.

There is also disagreement concerning the definition of naturalism, because some philosophers affirm the use of naturalism practically as method within scientific inquiry, and not as philosophy about the totality of reality. Papineau wrote, "In some philosophy of religion circles, 'methodological naturalism' is understood differently, as a thesis about natural scientific method itself, not about philosophical method."[2] *Oxford Dictionaries* defined naturalism: "A philosophical viewpoint according to which everything arises from natural properties and causes, and supernatural or spiritual explanations are excluded or discounted."[3] I will be arguing against naturalism as defined by *Oxford Dictionaries*. This type of naturalism goes beyond an empirical method of inquiry and includes a worldview or philosophy that is anti-supernatural and anti-theistic. This is the type of naturalism embraced by Peter Singer and Michael Tooley and seems to be implied by some of the other ethicists who defend abortion. Oxford biologist Richard Dawkins equates atheism with philosophical naturalism. He said:

> An atheist in the sense of a philosophical naturalist is somebody who believes that there is nothing beyond the natural, physical world, no supernatural creative intelligence lurking behind the observable universe, no soul that outlasts the body and no miracles—except in the

2   David Papineau, "Naturalism," *The Stanford Encyclopedia of Philosophy* (Spring 2009 Edition), retrieved at <http://plato.stanford.edu/archives/spr2009/entries/naturalism/>.

3   Oxford Dictionaries, "Naturalism," retrieved at http://www.oxforddictionaries.com/us/definition/american_english/naturalism.

sense of a natural phenomenon that we don't yet understand. If there is something that appears to lie beyond the natural world as it is now imperfectly understood, we hope eventually to understand it and embrace it within the natural. As ever when we unweave a rainbow, it will not become less wonderful.[4]

While some think that Singer's position is radical, others believe it is consistent with his utilitarianism and naturalism. Richard Dawkins interviewed Singer and said, "Peter, I think you must be one of the most moral people in the world. You've certainly got one of the most logically thought out ethical positions in the world."[5] Peter Singer's naturalism goes beyond a method of inquiry and also seems to be closely related to a philosophy of anti-theism. Singer wrote:

Here, as on many other moral issues, Christianity has for two thousand years been a powerful influence on the moral intuitions of people in Western societies. People do not need to continue to hold religious beliefs—for example, that God created the world, that he gave us dominion over the other animals, that we alone of all his creation have an immortal soul—the moral teachings just hang in the air, without foundations. If no better foundations can be

4   Richard Dawkins, *The God Delusion* (Boston: Houghton Mifflin Co. , 2006), 14.
5   "Peter Singer and The Genius of Darwin: The Uncut Interviews with Richard Dawkins" retrieved at http://www.youtube.com/watch?v=9xxdMUuZXUY.

provided for these teachings, we need to consider alternative views. So it is with the question of euthanasia, which, along with suicide has in non-Christian societies like ancient Rome and Japan been considered both a reasonable and an honorable way of ending one's life.[6]

I combine the word naturalism with materialism to refer to the worldview held by Peter Singer, that there are no supernatural causes, moral transcendence and nonphysical mind, but that everything in reality, including human beings, are purely material and physical. The *Stanford Encyclopedia of Philosophy* stated:

> Physicalism is sometimes known as "materialism"; indeed, on one strand of contemporary usage, the terms "physicalism" and "materialism" are interchangeable. Physicalism is the thesis that everything is physical, or as contemporary philosophers sometimes put it, that everything supervenes on, or is necessitated by, the physical. . . . The general idea is that the nature of the actual world (i.e. the universe and everything in it) conforms to a certain condition, the condition of being physical.[7]

Philosophers again may disagree concerning meaning and use of the words physicalism and materialism, so I

6   Peter Singer, *Writings On An Ethical Life* (New York: HarperCollins Publishers Inc., 2000), 32.
7   David Papineau, "Naturalism," *The Stanford Encyclopedia of Philosophy* (Spring 2009 Edition), retrieved at <http://plato.stanford.edu/archives/spr2009/entries/naturalism/>.

am using the word in a way that is closely related to the worldview of an anti-spiritual naturalism. Any explanation for metaphysical realities and especially concepts like mind, soul or supernatural are immediately rejected. Some naturalists may also embrace an idea that is closely related to the philosophy of *scientism,* which philosopher Steven Lehar defined as "the belief that science and its method of skeptical inquiry is the most reliable path to the truth."[8] However, with scientism there are a variety of definitions. Amongst naturalistic philosophers there is some debate about metaphysical realities and the levels of scientism or definition of scientism. J. P. Moreland wrote:

> Strong scientism is the view that some proposition or theory is true or rational if and only if it is a scientific proposition or theory. That is, if and only if it is a well-established scientific proposition or theory that, in turn, depends upon its having been successfully formed, tested, and used according to appropriate scientific methodology. There are no truths apart from scientific truths, and even if there were, there would be no reason whatever to believe them. . . . Weak scientism allows for the existence of truth apart from science and is even willing to grant that they can have some minimal, positive rationality status without the support of science. But, science is the most valuable, most serious, and most authoritative sector of

8   Steven Lehar, *Scientism: A System of Ethics Based on Reason Without Recourse to Supernatural Belief,* retrieved at Boston University's http://cns-alumni.bu.edu/~slehar/Scientism.pdf.

human learning. If strong scientism is true, then theology is not a rational enterprise at all and there is no such thing as theological knowledge. If weak scientism is true, then the conversation between theology and science will be a monologue with theology listening to science and waiting for science to give it support. For thinking Christians, neither of these alternatives is acceptable.[9]

Moreland indicates that strong scientism leaves no room for any immaterial reality or any type of transcendence, where weak scientism leaves open the possibility of immaterial realities and knowledge outside the scientific method. However, weak scientism still holds that the scientific method is the highest way of knowing reality. Although the terminology is not specifically claimed, it seems that strong scientism is assumed by some ethical defenders of abortion choice like Singer and Tooley, while perhaps a weaker form of scientism is embraced by Thomson and Boonin. A weaker form of scientism may adapt or change the ethical conclusions regarding the unborn baby. Perhaps this could be why Thomson wrote, "I propose, then that we grant that the fetus is a person from the moment of conception."[10] Peter Singer seems more committed to a stronger usage of scientism. He wrote, "Our nature is controlled by evolution, not by immutable divine command, so biologists rather than

9   J.P. Moreland, *Love God with All Your Mind*, (Colorado Springs: NavPress, 1997), 144–45.
10 Judith Jarvis Thomson, *Rights, Restitution & Risk* (Cambridge: Harvard University Press, 1986), 1.

theologians are the real authorities on what is natural for us."[11]

Some non-theistic philosophers believe that ethicists and scientists like Singer are speaking too dogmatically when endorsing a strong scientism coupled with naturalistic materialism as the only explanation of reality. Agnostic philosopher Thomas Nagel in his book *Mind and Cosmos: Why the Materialist Neo-Darwinian Conception of Nature is Almost Certainly False,* states, "But among the scientists and philosophers who do express views about the natural order as a whole, reductive materialism is widely assumed to be the only serious possibility."[12] Nagel argues that naturalism is not adequately answering all questions regarding mind, consciousness, and even origin. He wrote,

> It is prima facie highly implausible that life as we know it is the result of a sequence of physical accidents together with the mechanism of natural selection. We are expected to abandon this naïve response, not in favor of a fully worked out physical/chemical explanation but in favor of an alternative that is really a schema for explanation, supported by some examples. What is lacking, to my knowledge, is a credible argument that the story has a non-negligible probability of being true. There are two questions. First, given what is known about the

11 Singer, Peter, *The Expanding Circle: Ethics, Evolution, and Moral Progress* (Princeton: Princeton University Press, 2011), 58.

12 Thomas Nagel, *Mind and Cosmos: Why the Materialist Neo-Darwinian Conception of Nature is Almost Certainly False* (Oxford: Oxford Scholarship Online, 2013) 4.

chemical basis of biology and genetics, what is the likelihood that self-reproducing life forms should have come into existence spontaneously on the early earth, solely through the operation of the laws of physics and chemistry? The second question is about the sources of variation in the evolutionary process that was set in motion once life began: In the available geological time since the first life forms appeared on earth, what is the likelihood that, as a result of physical accident, a sequence of viable genetic mutations should have occurred that was sufficient to permit natural selection to produce the organisms that actually exist?[13]

Nagel has taken a different approach to the atheistic logical positivists of the twentieth century, like the Oxford philosopher A. J. Ayer who said, "If 'god' is a metaphysical term, then it cannot be even probable that a god exists. For to say that 'God exists' is to make a metaphysical utterance which cannot be either true or false."[14] Thomas Nagel, who does not affirm the existence of God, is not as dogmatic as Ayer and concludes that he *does not know*. William Lane Craig, a Christian philosopher, said:

Back in the 1940s and '50s, many philosophers believed that talk about God, since it is not verifiable by the five senses, is meaningless—actual nonsense. This verificationism finally collapsed,

13 Ibid.
14 A. J. Ayer, *Language, Truth, and Logic* (New York: Dover Publications, 1952), 115.

in part because philosophers realized that verificationism itself could not be verified! The collapse of verificationism was the most important philosophical event of the 20th century. Its downfall meant that philosophers were free once again to tackle traditional problems of philosophy that verificationism had suppressed."[15]

Because *scientism* is unverified, philosophers of science over the last fifty years have been leaving open the possibility of immaterial realities or at least admitting some level of agnosticism or scientism defined by weak scientism. Atheist philosopher Quentin Smith wrote:

> By the second half of the twentieth century, universities and colleges had been become [sic] in the main secularized. The standard (if not exceptionless) position in each field, from physics to psychology, assumed or involved arguments for a naturalist world-view; departments of theology or religion aimed to understand the meaning and origins of religious writings, not to develop arguments against naturalism. Analytic philosophers . . . treated theism as an anti-realist or non-cognitivist world-view, requiring the reality, not of a deity, but merely of emotive expressions or certain "forms of life." . . . Naturalists [have] passively watched as realist versions of theism, most influenced by Plantinga's

15 William Lane Craig, "Reasonable Faith" article retrieved at http://www.reasonablefaith.org/god-is-not-dead-yet#ixzz2nT7rNx00.

writings, began to sweep through the philosophical community, until today perhaps one-
quarter or one-third of philosophy professors
are theists, with most being orthodox Christians. . . . [I]n philosophy, it became, almost
overnight, "academically respectable" to argue
for theism, making philosophy a favored field
of entry for the most intelligent and talented
theists entering academia today. . . . God is not
"dead" in academia; he returned to life in the
late 1960s and is now alive and well in his last
academic stronghold, philosophy depart-
ments.[16]

While verification has now been rejected by many
philosophers of metaphysics, many ethical proponents of
abortion choice still assume this verification coupled with
scientism to be true. The reality of metaphysics has implications of what it means to be human and our knowledge
of how we should respect the good of other persons.

Is there a conflict between affirming science and believing in an immaterial reality? Some analytic philosophers argue that naturalism cannot explicitly show a
logical contradiction between affirming science (including
evolution) and God. Christian philosopher Alvin Plantinga says, "There is no real conflict between theistic religion and the scientific theory of evolution. What there is,
instead, is conflict between theistic religion and a philosophical gloss or add-on to the scientific doctrine of evolution: the claim that evolution is undirected, unguided,

16 Quentin Smith, "The Metaphilosophy of Naturalism," *Philo* 4, no.
2 (2001): 3–4.

unorchestrated by God (or anyone else)."[17] The existence of God could be an adequate explanation for the existence of materials that allowed evolution to happen. Plantinga argues that there is a conflict between naturalism and evolution. He wrote:

> Taking naturalism to include materialism with respect to human beings, I argue that it is improbable, given naturalism and evolution, that our cognitive faculties are reliable. It is improbable that they provide us with a suitable preponderance of true belief over false.[18]

Many naturalistic materialists are dependent on the sole existence of evolution combined with strong scientism. Strong scientism combined with naturalistic materialism is not able to account for transcendence. However, if an immaterial mind is a fundamental reality, one can make sense of levels of consciousness and the existence of personal minds evolving through a process to reach a state where one obtains accurate knowledge of other persons.

In this section we began by saying that Peter Singer is an example of a defender of abortion, who is committed to a philosophy of naturalism or strong scientism. This strict naturalistic materialism combined with strong scientism leaves no room for any immaterial reality or any type of transcendence. Weaker commitments to naturalistic materialism leave open the possibility of knowing the existence of "transcendence," "dignity," and "rights" that

17 Plantinga, Alvin, *Where the Conflict Really Lies: Science, Religion, and Naturalism* (New York: Oxford University Press, 2011), xii.
18 Ibid.

go beyond the laboratory and the scientific method. Science alone cannot judge the rightness or wrongness of an action done to a human being because science does not speak for itself—scientists speak on behalf of science. Scientists, too, hold metaphysical assumptions about reality.

Chapter 6.

The Terms "Sanctity" and "Natural Theology" Should Not Necessarily Be Dismissed in Philosophy or Law Because It Might Have Implications of the Divine

Peter Singer in his book *Unsanctifying Human Life* said:

> The challenge to theological doctrines that gave rise to the doctrine of the sanctity of human life has, by and large, succeeded. The challenge to the moral attitudes themselves has made slower progress. Laws against abortion have been substantially weakened or abolished in many countries, but a doctor may still be charged with murder if he kills an infant, no matter how retarded. My brief historical survey suggests that the intuitions which lie behind these laws are not insights of self-evident moral truths, but the historically conditioned product of doctrines about immortality, original sin, and damnation which hardly anyone now accepts; doctrines so obnoxious, in fact, that if anyone did accept them, we should be inclined to discount any other moral views he held. Although advocates of the doctrine of the sanctity of human life now

> frequently try to give their position some secular justification, there can be no possible justification for making the boundary of sanctity run parallel with the boundary of our own species, unless we invoke some belief about immortal souls.[1]

Yet Singer is condemning the ideas held by *not* just "hardly anyone," but potentially an estimated *two billion people* who follow the world's largest religion, Christianity. Singer believes that an ethicist who held to Christianity is obnoxious and that "we should be inclined to discount any other moral views he held."

Peter Singer said, "People do not need to continue to hold religious beliefs—for example, that God created the world."[2] Yet he did not provide foundations or adequate arguments for his naturalistic atheism that rules out a great tradition of natural theology. Singer also accuses the ethics of Christianity of being a "Western tradition."[3] In response, the ethics of Christianity is not merely a Western tradition. The movement started in the east. Jesus and many of the writers of the New Testament, like the apostle Paul, were Aramaic.

There have been naturalistic arguments for God's existence provided by philosophers outside the Judeo-Christian tradition, such as those provided by Muslim philosophers like Avicenna, Averroes and Al-Ghazali in the middle ages. Singer does not fully reveal a rebuttal of philosophers of natural theology. However, he claims that moral teachings of creation "just hang in the air,

---

1   Peter Singer, *Unsanctifying Human Life*, ed. Helga Kuhse (Oxford: Blackwell Publishers, 2002), 230.

2   Peter Singer, *Writings on an Ethical Life* (New York: HarperCollins Publishers Inc., 2000), 32.

3   Ibid., *xviii*.

without foundations."[4] Charles Taliaferro defines Natural Theology as the "practice of philosophically reflecting on the existence and nature of God independent of real or apparent divine revelation or scripture."[5] Some naturalistic ethicists and atheistic naturalists believe that speaking about God is fine for the churchgoer, but assert that the realm of faith is not related to knowledge and should not be addressed in philosophy or politics. Dawkins, who affirms Singer's naturalistic ethics, stated, "Faith is the great cop-out, the great excuse to evade and need to think and evaluate evidence. Faith is the belief in spite of, even perhaps because of lack of evidence."[6] In response, there is a distinction between faith and Natural Theology. Natural Theology speaks of truths known by *reason*. Although some existentialists like Soren Kierkegaard (1813–1855) regard faith as contrary to

---

4   Ibid., 32.
5   Charles Taliaferro, *The Blackwell Companion of Natural Theology*, ed. William Lane Craig and J. P. Moreland (Oxford: Blackwell Publishing, 2009), 1.
6   Richard Dawkins cited in Alister E. McGrath, *Christianity: An Introduction* (Oxford, Blackwell Publishing, 2006), 102.
7   Kierkegaard, "[A person should] relinquish his understanding and his thinking, to keep his soul fixed upon the absurd." Soren Kierkegaard, trans. David F. Swenson and Walter Lowrie, *Concluding Unscientific Postscript* (Princeton, NJ: Princeton University Press, 1941), 495. Kierkegaard, "[Christians should reach a] crucifixion of the understanding." Soren Kierkegaard, trans. David F. Swenson and Walter Lowrie, *Concluding Unscientific Postscript* (Princeton, NJ: Princeton University Press, 1941), 496. Kierkegaard, "Belief [faith] is not a form of knowledge but a free act, an expression of the will . . . the conclusion of belief is not so much a conclusion but a resolution." Soren Kierkegaard, trans. David Swenson and Howard V. Hong, *Philosophical Fragments or a Fragment of Philosophy* (Princeton, NJ: Princeton University Press, 1962), 103–4.

intellect,[7] there is a great tradition, beginning in early Christianity, that both grounds faith in evidence and says natural theology is narrower than faith, based solely on reason.[8] Faith may apply to truths given in special revelation such as the Bible's description of the Trinity, the Virgin Birth, or the Second Coming of Christ, but that is emphatically *not* what we are talking about in regard to natural theology. Historically, from the time of Socrates to recent philosophers like Plantinga, philosophy has frequently addressed the reality of God without appeals to special revelation. Taliaferro wrote:

> Plato (428–348 BCE), Aristotle (384–322 BCE) and their successors in ancient and medieval philosophy developed substantial arguments for the existence of God without relying on revelation. In the West, Anselm of Canterbury (1033–1109), Thomas Aquinas (1225–74), and Duns Scotus (1266–1308) are among the most celebrated contributors to natural theology. Muslim philosophy has also been a rich resource for natural theology, especially for cosmological theistic arguments. This may be due, in part, to the immense emphasis by philosophers such as Ibn Sina (or Avicenna, 980–1037) on the necessary, noncontingent reality of God in contrast to the contingent cosmos. Natural theology played a major role in early modern

8   "Now faith is the substance of things hoped for, the evidence of things not seen." (Hebrews 11:1 KJV) The Christian notion of faith goes beyond natural theology. However, the Christian notion of faith historically was not always "blind" in the way that Dawkins describes.

philosophy. Some of the classics in the modern era, such as *Meditations* by Descartes (1596–1650), *An Essay Concerning Human Understanding* by John Locke (1632–1704), *Three Dialogues between Hylas and Philonous* by George Berkeley, the *Theodicy* by Leibniz (1646–1716), the *Dialogues Concerning Natural Religion* by David Hume (1711–76), and the *Critique of Pure Reason* by Immanuel Kant (1724–1804), all constitute major contributions to assessing reasons for and against theism, without making any appeal to revelation.[9]

Peter Kreeft said, "There have been at least two dozen very different sorts of attempts to prove the existence of God."[10] What is disappointing is that the leading advocates of abortion choice who dismiss natural theology do not say why they reject arguments for a transcendent being like God. If there is something of transcendence that really does exist, this has implications of dignity. Peter Singer dismissed arguments for God's existence as irrelevant and an "inadequate foundation." I will briefly mention just three reasons for the existence of God. Two of the ways are from Aquinas, and though they do not provide a full description of the properties theologians use to describe God, these ways do reveal several key attributes of what we mean by God. However, these reasons do not appeal to some sacred book or literature, but are rather

9   Charles Taliaferro, *The Blackwell Companion of Natural Theology*, ed. William Lane Craig and J. P. Moreland (Oxford: Blackwell Publishing, 2009), 1.

10 Thomas Aquinas, *Summa of the Summa*, ST I, q 2, a 3. edited and annotated by Peter Kreeft (San Francisco: Ignatius Press, 1990), 63.

philosophical arguments, with premises that appeal to un-aided reason leading to a conclusion.

God is the best explanation for a first efficient cause.
Thomas Aquinas's second way states:

> In the world of sense we find there is an order
> of efficient causes. There is no case known (nei-
> ther is it, indeed, possible) in which a thing is
> found to be the efficient cause of itself; for so it
> would be prior to itself, which is impossible.
> Now in efficient causes it is not possible to go
> on to infinity, because in all efficient causes fol-
> lowing in order, the first is the cause of the in-
> termediate cause, and the intermediate is the
> cause of the ultimate cause, whether the inter-
> mediate cause be several, or one only. Now to
> take away the cause is to take away the effect.
> Therefore, if there be no first cause among effi-
> cient causes, there will be no ultimate, nor any
> intermediate cause. But if in efficient causes it is
> possible to go on to infinity, there will be no first
> efficient causes; all of which is plainly false.
> Therefore it is necessary to admit a first efficient
> cause, to which everyone gives the name God.[11]

Aquinas, borrowing terminology from Aristotle, begins
with his senses to appeal to an order in the universe and
an order in causality. He *never* states "Everything needs a
cause." Edward Feser wrote, "He begins the argument by
saying there are efficient causes and that nothing can

11   Ibid., 66.

cause itself. The implication is that if something is caused, then it is something outside the thing being caused that is doing the causing."[12] Aquinas's second way is different from the Kalam argument defended by the Islamic philosopher Al-Ghazali (1058–1111), which appeals to the beginning of the universe. Aquinas's argument does not seek to answer whether the universe is eternal or temporal. Aquinas appealed to the causality in relationship with things. He wrote about the relationship of causes now. Perhaps, even the skeptic David Hume would not dogmatically reject this point. For Hume said:

> I never asserted so absurd a proposition that any thing might arise without Cause. I only maintained, that our Certainty of the Falsehood of that Proposition proceeded neither from Intuition nor Demonstration; but from another Source.[13]

Hume, the skeptic, asserted that our senses do not provide us with certain knowledge regarding causality, but he was not rejecting its existence altogether. Aquinas believed, empirically, that humans observe with the senses but make judgments with the mind. The contemporary atheist Dawkins misrepresents this principle of causality by asking, "Who made God?" This is a category mistake. As a theologian, Aquinas is not saying that everything needs a cause. Only finite things need a cause. God is what all men mean to be an uncaused Cause. Aquinas is referring

12 Edward Feser, *Aquinas* (Oxford, One World Publications, 2009), 80.
13 David Hume's *Letter to Stewart*, Hume Studies Volume 1, retrieved at http://www.humesociety.org/.

to an essentially ordered series, a causal series that entails each entity to be in place for the end to work. This second way has implications closely related to what Aquinas wrote about it in his *On Being and Essence*. Aquinas distinguished between essence and existence. Essence is *what a thing is*. Existence is the actuality of an essence, the act by which something really is. Aquinas believed that essence and existence are distinct. It's not in the nature of things to exist. They must be brought into existence by something else. Although we will not address all of Aquinas's five ways, this is also closely related to the first way which addressed the relationship of actualizing the potentiality of something else. The first way showed a something that was pure act and immaterial. The second way by Aquinas provided a reason to believe in a first cause.

God is the best explanation for a necessary entity.
Thomas Aquinas's Third Way argues that contingent beings depend on a Necessary Being.

> We find in nature things that are possible to be and not to be, since they are found to be generated, and to corrupt, and consequently, they are possible to be and not to be. But it is impossible for these always to exist, for that which is possible not to be at some time is not. Therefore, if everything is possible not to be, then at one time there could have been nothing in existence. Now if this were true, even now there would be nothing in existence, because that which does not exist only begins to exist by something already existing. Therefore, if at one time nothing was in existence, it would have been impossible

for anything to have begun to exist; and thus even now nothing would be in existence— which is absurd. Therefore, not all beings are merely possible, but there must exist something the existence of which is necessary. But every necessary thing either has its necessity caused by another or not. Now it is impossible to go on to infinity in necessary things which have their necessity caused by another, as has been already proved in regard to efficient causes. Therefore we cannot but postulate the existence of some being having of itself its own necessity, and not receiving it from another, but rather causing in others their necessity. This all men speak of as God.[14]

According to Thomas Aquinas, the word *contingent* means things that can exist or not exist, things like trees, stones and animals. *Necessary* means that which cannot be otherwise, or that which has permanent existence. Aquinas is arguing that there must be a necessary being who does not depend on anything else for its existence. There are some contemporary naturalistic philosophers focusing on symbolic logic who misrepresent Aquinas's Third Way. Edward Feser observed:

In short, the Third Way holds that the world of contingent things could not exist at all unless there were a necessary being. It would be a serious mistake, however, to understand "contingent" and "necessary" here in the senses most

14 Thomas Aquinas, *ST* I, q 2, a 3.

> familiar to contemporary philosophers, many of whom think (for example) of what is necessary as that which exists only in some possible worlds, or who assume that the notion of a necessary being must be that of a being the denial of the existence of which would entail of self-contradiction.[15]

Aquinas is not talking about possible and impossible in the symbolic "possible" world sense. Beings that exist and are also contingent really do exist, but who may not exist because their nature may have an inherent tendency towards corruption. When Aquinas speaks of a necessary being, he is talking about a being who cannot *not* exist. Aquinas is affirming that human beings can have knowledge of this reality about the Being who by nature must exist.

God is the best explanation for moral realism.
Although those in favor of abortion may disagree about when it's okay to kill a human being and when it's not okay, these same advocates for abortion choice would agree amongst themselves (and of course with the vast majority of pro-lifers) that it was really wrong for Scott Roeder to shoot late-term abortionist George Tiller, who was serving as an usher at Reformation Lutheran Church in Wichita, Kansas on May 31, 2009. The majority of both scholarly pro-life and pro-abortion philosophers are moral realists.

Atheist Evan Fales wrote, "Moral realism is the view, roughly, that moral norms are not simply 'made up' by

15   Edward Feser, *Aquinas* (Oxford: One World Publications, 2009), 90.

people: their existence isn't a matter of what someone or some group thinks they are."[16] This is closely related to the phrase "objective moral law." The word "objective" indicates the existence of something that is independent of a person's perception of it. A notion of objectivity applied to moral law would imply that some things are right and wrong, regardless of what people intend or regardless of the end results. However, more broadly speaking, notions of objectivity could be applied to systems of ethics that are deontological or duty-centered as with Immanuel Kant's, as well as some virtue ethical systems following Aristotle that are teleological in nature, emphasizing consistent ends and consistent means. Even utilitarianism (i.e., Mill, Bentham and Singer) seems to have a minimum appeal to objectivity, appealing to pragmatic end results or to the maximum amount of pleasure and avoidance of pain for the maximum amount of people.

The opposite of moral realism could be called moral non-realism. Frequently a moral non-realist will also hold the view of moral relativism. Chris Gowans defined moral relativism in the *Stanford Encyclopedia of Philosophy* by stating that "the truth or justification of moral judgments is not absolute, but relative to some group of persons."[17] On the other hand, a moral realist would reject relativism and hold that it was objectively wrong for southerners to own slaves before the Civil War, even though the majority in some southern communities believed that owning slaves was morally permissible. A moral relativist might claim

16   Evan Fales, *God & Morality: Four Views*, ed. R. Keith Loftin (Downers Grove, Illinois: IVP Academic, 2012), 14.

17   Chris Gowans, "Moral Relativism", *The Stanford Encyclopedia of Philosophy* (Spring 2012 Edition) accessed at http://plato.stanford.edu/archives/spr2012/entries/moral-relativism/>.

that it was only relatively wrong, but not objectively wrong. Most scholarly abortion choice defenders would hold to some form of moral realism, believing that there is at minimum one objective moral law transcending time and cultures. For example, Peter Singer agrees that relativism is self-defeating. Singer wrote, "The fourth, and last, claim about ethics that I shall deny in the chapter is that ethics is relative or subjective."[18]

One of the ways some theists argue for the existence of God is by arguing that the existence of God provides the best explanation for moral essentialism, that is, that some moral laws are objectively true for all people, at all times and all places. One version of the argument states:

1. If God does not exist, then objective moral truths do not exist.
2. Objective moral truths do exist.
3. Therefore, God exists.

Premise one seems to be rejected by some atheists who affirm the truth of the second premise. They appeal to atheists having epistemological knowledge of moral truths and do not need a God. Peter Singer wrote:

> There are no moral principles that are shared by all religious people, regardless of their specific beliefs, but by no agnostics and atheists. Indeed, atheists and agnostics do not behave less morally than religious believers, even if their virtuous acts rest on different principles. Nonbelievers often have as strong and sound a

18 Peter Singer, *Writings on an Ethical Life* (New York: HarperCollins Publishers Inc., 2000), xv.

sense of right and wrong as anyone, and have
worked to abolish slavery and contributed to
other efforts to alleviate human suffering.[19]

I think Singer is correct in affirming that atheists and ag-
nostics affirm the moral principles like the golden rule
that is shared by all religious people. But let me make two
important clarifications in reply to Singer. The moral argument for God's existence is not stating that atheists cannot be moral people. Secondly, the first premise is not
claiming that atheists do not know and understand moral
truths. The first premise is appealing to ontological
grounding, not epistemological awareness.

Atheist philosopher Evan Fales, who rejected premise
one, holds the position of naturalist moral realism. He has
described his position as follows: "Both naturalism and
realism are contested terms. For present purposes, I will
take naturalism to involve, minimally, a commitment to
there being no disembodied minds."[20] Fales seeks to defend ontologically *why* there is no need of God for objectivity in ethics, appealing to ancient principles of
teleology. I certainly believe that it would be a step in the
right direction if more pro-abortion ethicists would embrace a moral essentialism in a way similar to Fales's.
Fales wrote:

> I am going to insist that intrinsic teleological
> properties are to be found in the natural world:

19 Peter Singer and Mac Hauser, "Godless Morality," *Project Syndicate*
    (January 2006) accessed at http://www.project-syndicate.org/
    commentary/godless-morality.
20 Evan Fales, *God & Morality: Four Views*, ed. R. Keith Loftin, (Down-
    ers Grove, Illinois: IVP Academic, 2012), 17.

there are natural ITOSs [Intelligent Teleological Organized Systems]. Nor must an ITOS be conscious: intrinsic teleology can be found in systems that do not possess consciousness. An acorn's *telos* is to grow into an oak. An oak tree's *teloi* are to flourish (in an oakish sort of way) and to produce more acorns. It is plain, and open to empirical inspection, whether an oak achieves these ends or whether it does not—and that it *has* these ends—as the tree's branches or its height. These are all equally natural features of the oak.[21]

Fales does make some good observations adapted from classical notions of teleology. As a side comment pertaining to our thesis topic of human beings, it seems that these intrinsic properties of ITOSes correlate with notions of intrinsic unity and intrinsic *teloi* within human babies well. If Fales is correct, an embryo has *teloi* to develop into a newborn child, just as a kindergarten student has *teloi* to develop into a college student. However, there is a unity even if these ends are ever accomplished.

Fales's understanding of *telos* is adapted from Aristotle, but he still does not adequately explain *why* such notions of *telos* exist in reality, nor does he defend the particular subject of morality. Aristotle did not appeal to an unmoved mover in his ethics as he did in his metaphysics. However, Aristotle seemed to take a broader view of philosophy, in which the fields of metaphysics and ethics may be connected rather than completely

21 Ibid.

separated. Aristotle's philosophy of all reality was teleological, but to account for the existence of all that exists in reality, he affirmed a principle on which "depend the heavens and the world of nature."[22] Aristotle said, "The first mover, then, exists of necessity; and in so far as it exists by necessity, its mode of being is good, and it is in this sense a first principle."[23] Fales wrote:

> In my view, the ethical naturalist ought to respond to the question, Why be moral? in very much the same vein as Plato and Aristotle. However acquired, we have souls (in the ancient Greek sense), so ordered that virtue is its own reward—more precisely, it provides the greatest rewards a soul can enjoy.[24]

Although Fales is correct that one who can apprehend the reality of teleology does not have to believe in God, he still does not adequately explain why objective *moral* truths like virtue really do exist. Fales added, "(N)or can I hope to do better than Plato and Aristotle themselves."[25] It seems Fales ignored some of the overall implications of the entirety of Plato's and Aristotle's philosophy. Plato, whose philosophy was quite distinct from Aristotle, affirmed the Good, which was immaterial and eternal. Aristotle did not did see God as the natural law giver as Thomas Aquinas would later argue. However, Aristotle still affirmed the existence of an unmoved mover who

22 Aristotle, *Metaphysics*, 12.7.
23 Ibid.
24 Evan Fales, *God & Morality: Four Views*, ed. R. Keith Loftin (Downers Grove, Illinois: IVP Academic, 2012), 20–21.
25 Ibid., 21.

"compels our wonder."[26] The relationship between God and ethics is not explicit but could be implicit considering the existence and movement of actuality of thought, according to Aristotle:

> If, then, God is always in that good state in which we sometimes are, this compels our wonder; and if in a better this compels it yet more. And God is in a better state. And life also belongs to God; for the actuality of thought is life, and God is that actuality; and God's self-dependent actuality is life most good and eternal.[27]

Atheist Michael Ruse argued that Fales is being inconsistent with his atheism by also appealing to Aristotle's teleological notions and combining them with atheistic naturalism. Ruse quoted Richard Dawkins in response to Fales, "The universe we observe has precisely the properties we should expect if there is, at bottom, no design, no purpose, no evil and no good, nothing but blind, pitiless indifference."[28] If it is true that the world of evolution is blind, then I think Ruse is correct; there would be no objective purpose, no evil and no good. But if there exists a transcendent mind or some sort of moral law giver, the existence of such an entity could be a *better explanation* of why there are objective moral laws than that provided by atheistic naturalism. The argument that we referenced earlier stated:

26 Aristotle, *Metaphysics*, 12.7.
27 Ibid.
28 Richard Dawkins, *River Out of Eden*, 133, cited by Michael Ruse, *God & Morality: Four Views*, ed. R. Keith Loftin (Downers Grove, Illinois: IVP Academic, 2012), 38.

1. If God does not exist, then objective moral truths do not exist.
2. Objective moral truths do exist.
3. Therefore, God exists.

Premise two is affirmed by the majority of scholarly defenders of abortion, but rejected by many sociologists and cultural defenders of abortion. Atheist philosopher Michael Ruse affirms premise one. However he rejects premise two, appealing to Darwin and Hume. Yet he believes that for pragmatic purposes it would be good for people to live as if premise two were true. He wrote:

> If I am right philosophically, then there is no absolute, objective basis to morality. I am talking about how we feel and what we mean. In other words, I am talking about our psychology, if you like. My position is exactly that of David Hume when he claimed that his philosophical inquiries led him to skepticism, but that after a while back in the real world (playing backgammon and so forth) his psychology took over and he didn't bother about skepticism. Just as for Hume and his skepticism about the world, there are obvious Darwinian reasons why we should thus "objectivize" morality. If we knew that morality was subjective and that we could ignore it, then very quickly morality would break down and people would start cheating and before long there would be general mayhem. But because we think that morality is objective, we all obey it more or less. In other words, I'm saying it is a Darwinian adaptation that we should

be deceived about the justificatory status of morality. Morality may have no foundation, but it is in our biological interests that we should think that it has. Hence, we do think that it has.[29]

But if this is true, murdering an abortionist like Tiller is not objectively, absolutely, morally wrong. Neither is anything, including gang rape and genocide, *really* wrong according to Ruse's position. If we are only obeying these principles because of our moral adaptation, then how are we to know what to do when humans and other animals adapt in contrary ways? Perhaps Ruse's position is more consistent with atheistic naturalism than Fales's. William Lane Craig stated:

> But if atheism is true, what basis is there for the objectivity of the moral values we affirm? Evolution? Social conditioning? These factors may at best produce in us the subjective *feeling* that there are objective moral values and duties, but they do nothing to provide a basis for them. If human evolution had taken a different path, a very different set of moral feelings might have evolved.[30]

The existence of objective moral truths could lead us to think about certain options concerning why these moral

29 Michael Ruse, *God & Morality: Four Views*, ed. R. Keith Loftin (Downers Grove, Illinois: IVP Academic, 2012), 55.
30 William Lane Craig, "A Christmas gift for atheists—five reasons why God exists." Retrieved on http://www.foxnews.com/opinion.

goods exists. Plato believed in the preexistent, eternal world of the forms. Aristotle rejected dualistic separation of the physical world and the world of the forms. However, Plato seemed correct in his awareness of *something* being transcendent and unchanging.

For simplicity, it seems that if something transcendent like Good exists, then one can make a case why murdering another human being is objectively wrong. By the notion of objectivity in ethics, we mean that this law is prescribed to all people, and not just subjective to particular cultures or individuals. However, if this law is prescribed to all human beings, there must be *some* prescriber. If there is a law written on hearts, there must be a writer. Some laws seem objective and related to a Supreme Ruler. Augustine wrote, "That law which is the supreme reason cannot be understood to be otherwise than unchangeable and eternal."[31] The terms "unchangeable" and "eternal" are consistent with the theistic notion of God. C. S. Lewis wrote:

> Something which is directing the universe and which appears in me as a law is urging me to do right and making me feel responsible and uncomfortable when I do wrong. I think we have to assume it is more like a mind than it is like anything else we know—because after all the only other thing we know is matter and you can hardly imagine a bit of matter giving instructions."[32]

31 Augustine, *De Lib.* Arb. 1.6 cited by Thomas Aquinas, *Summa Theologica*, 2.91.1
32 C. S. Lewis, *Mere Christianity* (New York: Harper Collins, 1952), 26.

Lewis believed that this something was more like a mind, or someone. In addition to Lewis, some atheists have believed that there was some sort of connection with moral laws and a being like God, whom they do not want reminding them how to act. Jean-Paul Sartre described having an experience as a child:

> I had been playing with matches and burned a small rug. I was in the process of covering up my crime when suddenly God saw me. I felt His gaze inside my head and on my hands . . . . I flew into a rage against so crude an indiscretion, I blasphemed. . . . He never looked at me again. . . . I had the more difficulty getting rid of Him [the Holy Ghost] in that He had installed Himself at the back of my head. . . . I collared the Holy Ghost in the cellar and threw Him out.[33]

Sartre appears honest in believing in a concept of consciousness that experiences guilt and anger while disobeying the Giver of moral laws. Abortion defender Peter Singer rejects the notion that we need God for moral principles, while also appealing to the ethics of Thomas Jefferson, one of America's founding fathers. Singer wrote:

> Thomas Jefferson, who was responsible for writing the principle of the equality of men into the American Declaration of Independence, saw this point. It led him to oppose slavery even

---

33 Jean-Paul Sartre, *The Words* (New York: George Braziller, 1964), 102, 252–53.

though he was unable to free himself fully from
his slaveholding background. He wrote in a letter to the author of a book that emphasized the
notable intellectual achievements of Negros in
order to refute the then common view that they
had limited intellectual capacities.[34]

Although Singer and some other naturalists appeal to the
deist Jefferson for their utilitarianism, Jefferson believed
that some of these rights were endowed by God. He wrote
in the Declaration of Independence, "We hold these truths
to be self-evident, that all men are created equal, that they
are endowed by their Creator with certain unalienable
Rights, that among these are Life, Liberty and the Pursuit
of Happiness." Singer praises Jefferson for believing that
all men are created equal, but Jefferson's declaration also
says that they are "endowed by their Creator." Although
Jefferson did not argue that God was explicitly the ontological reason for all objective moral laws, he saw some
connection to the Creator as the one who endows the *right
to life*. At least, we could say that some objective moral
prescriptions, whether these are "rights" or "laws written
on the heart," can best be explained if there were some
moral prescriber. Thomas Aquinas wrote,

> Those things that are not in themselves, exist
> with God, in as much as they are foreknown
> and preordained by Him, according to Romans
> 4:17: 'Who calls those things that are not, as
> those that are.' Accordingly the eternal concept

34 Peter Singer, *Writings on an Ethical Life* (New York: HarperCollins
Publishers Inc., 2000), 32.

of the Divine law bears the character of an eternal law, in so far as it is ordained by God to the government of things foreknown by Him.[35]

In conclusion, it does seem there is an eternal law, that exists in God, that both the divine law and natural law are related to. If this eternal immaterial mind does not exist, then there are not adequate ontological reasons to affirm the existence of objective moral truths. Moral norms that are objective are more like laws and cannot simply be "made up" by people. The existence of these moral laws and prescriptions imply a moral-law giver, who is an eternal, immaterial mind, that I call God.

35 Thomas Aquinas, *Summa Theologica*, 2.91.1

Chapter 7.

Aristotle's Ancient Concept of Substance Is Still Relevant and Compatible with Science.

The classical notion of substance literally means to "stand under." A substance is something that exists in itself, not in another.

Aristotle wrote:

> A substance—that which is called a substance most strictly, primarily, and most of all—is that which is neither said of a subject nor in a subject, e.g. the individual man or the individual horse. The species in which the things primarily called substances are, are called secondary substances, as also are the genera of these species. For example, the individual man belongs in a species, man, and animal is a genus of the species; so these—both man and animal—are called secondary substances.[1]

A substance is a unity of form and matter. Peter Kreeft described how the Aristotelian concept of matter is distinct from our modern understanding of matter. He wrote:

1   Aristotle *Categories* 2a13 (translated by J. L. Ackrill).

(Matter is) the principle in a thing's being by which it is able to be determined by form; potency as vs. actuality. In modern parlance, the word refers to actual, visible, formed things (e.g., chemicals, molecules); but in Thomistic and Aristotelian parlance "matter" is not of itself observable or even of itself actual. It is not a thing but a metaphysical principle or aspect of things, which together with form explains change, as the actualization (in-form-ing) of potency (matter).[2]

Dr. William Lawhead summarizes these Aristotelian concepts that Peter Kreeft described:

The "whatness" refers to its form. Its "thisness" is its matter. The easiest way to see how these two features work together to constitute individual realities is to consider a simple object such as a coffee cup. We can answer the question "What is it?" because we recognize that the object has a particular form. In this case, it is an object that is cylindrical, about three inches in diameter, with a closed bottom and an open top, which is used to drink coffee. Even though many such objects are mass-produced with the same form its matter lets us identify *this* cup as an individual reality of its own because it is this particular piece of formed ceramic sitting on my breakfast table.[3]

2 Peter Kreeft, *Summa of the Summa* (San Francisco: Ignatius Press, 1990), 27.
3 William F. Lawhead, *Voyage of Discovery* (Belmont: Wadsworth/ Thomas Learning, 2002), 76.

Lawhead continues:

> This particular example may lead us to suppose
> that form and matter refer to physical shape and
> physical matter alone. However, certain sub-
> tleties in Aristotle's account must be under-
> stood. Broadly speaking, an object has the form
> it has because of a particular purpose or func-
> tion it serves. The form constitutes an object's
> essence. The essence of something is the set of
> qualities that make it the sort of thing it is. Typ-
> ically, the essence of a thing is what a dictionary
> attempts to describe. For example, the essence
> of a coffee cup is to hold coffee so that we can
> drink from it. Hence, even if an object had the
> physical shape of a cup but was made from sol-
> uble material, it might be a decoration or an
> item in a practical joker's inventory, but it
> wouldn't really be a coffee cup. A coffee cup has
> an open top because its function is to serve bev-
> erages, whereas a juice bottle has a secure cap
> because its function is to store and transport
> beverages.[4]

The first of Aristotle's ten categories is substance, which
is distinct from the nine other categories which are called
accidents. Not only are these categories in the mind, but
categories in extramental reality. Aristotle's concepts of
accidents refer to the mode of being which can only exist
in another being like the blondeness or blackness of hair
or the redness of a nose. A substance according to Aristotle

---

4   Ibid.

is that which answers the question, "What is it?" For example, the answer may be Dave Sterrett, a particular man. If we were to ask:

* "How large is it?" (Quantity)
  Answer: Six feet, seven inches tall, 225 pounds.

* "What is it like?" (Quality)
  Answer: Athletic and outgoing.

* "How is it related?" (Relation)
  Answer: Shorter than NBA basketball player Lebron James.

* "Where is it?" (Place)
  Answer: In Staunton, Virginia.

* "When does it exist?" (Time)
  Answer: Today.

* "What position is it in?" (Position)
  Answer: Sitting.

* "What condition is it in?" (State)
  Answer: Clothed (thankfully).

* "What is it doing?" (Action)
  Answer: Typing on a computer.

* "How is it being acted on?" (Passivity)
  Answer: Being pushed out of his chair by his pet Great Dane.

Joseph Owens wrote, "The sole absolutely basic essence of finite things is called its substance."[5] A first substance would be an individual man like me, Dave Sterrett, not a general concept of "man." George Klubertantz said, "First substance is not predicament at all, because it is never a predicate. The first substance is a singular substance which exists. When we want to designate the being precisely as an existing, substantial, complete individual, we call it a 'supposit.'"[6] Robert Spaemann argues:

> The person does not begin its existence after the human being, nor does it end its existence before the human being. To speak of potential persons is meaningless, furthermore, because the concept of potentiality itself can arise only on the supposition of the underlying personality. Persons are, or they are not. If they *are*, they are *actual*. They are like Aristotelian "substance," or first reality which contains in itself the possibility of a multitude of further actualizations.[7]

W. Norris Clarke defines a human substance:

> (1) it has the aptitude to exist in itself and not as a part of any other being; (2) it is the unifying

---

5   Joseph Owens, *An Elementary Christian Metaphysics*, 154., cited by Howe, Thomas 1991. "Toward a Thomistic Theory of Meaning." Master's Thesis Liberty University.

6   George Klubertanz, *Introduction to the Philosophy of Being*, (New York: Meredith Publishing Company, 1963), 251.

7   Robert Spaemann, *Persons: The Difference Between "Something" and "Something"* (New York: Oxford University Press, 2006).

center of all the various attributes and properties that belong to it at any one moment; (3) if the being persists as the same individual throughout a process of change, it is the substance which is the abiding, unifying center of the being across time; (4) it has an intrinsic dynamic orientation toward self-expressive action, toward self-communication with others, as the crown of its perfection, as its very *raison d'etre*.[8]

I mentioned myself as an example of a substance. Yet there was a time in which I, Dave Sterrett, was a twelve-year-old boy who was only five feet tall. My physical accidents have changed, but my substance remains. The substance view says that there is a unity between the personhood and nature of a human being. Now, at the age of 33, I am a 6 feet and 7 inches tall man. I have moved locations and grown in knowledge, but I am still the same Dave Sterrett. However, many critics believe that one's essence comes out of existence depending upon the proper function. No doubt, there is a big *physical* difference between a child and a grown adult or an acorn and an oak tree. Obviously the latter in each case is much bigger and fully mature; however, the substance of each remains the same. Let's consider another example, a barking dog. The barking of the dog is a function that is normative to a vast majority of dogs. However, if a defective dog is born without the ability to bark, it still remains a dog. The substance view transcends mere physical matter and though it's distinct

---

8   W. Norris Clarke, *Explorations in Metaphysics* (Notre Dame, IN: University of Notre Dame Press, 1994), 105. Cited by Francis Beckwith, *Defending Life* (Cambridge, Cambridge University Press, 2007), 132.

from pure biological matter, it is not separate from it. Plato— and later Berkeley—emphasized that only the immaterial is truly real, but the substance view according to Aristotle and Aquinas has a unity with the physical.

This substance view is non-contradictory to empirical observations, including the theory of biogenesis, which states that living things can only arise from living things and cannot be spontaneously generated. Although the human body is constantly changing and cells are dying and being replaced, one's identity goes beyond mere cells. An embryo does not look like a newborn baby, nor does a newborn baby look like a teenager, nor does a teenager look like an elderly human. Biogenesis implies that each species reproduces after its own kind. An embryo does not begin with one species and then transform into another species. Biologically, many in favor of abortion choice affirm some sort of a physiological unity continuing throughout one's life. Peter Singer said,

> Whether a being is a member of a given species is something that can be determined scientifically, by an examination of the nature of the chromosomes in the cells of the living organisms. In this sense there is no doubt that from the first moments of its existence an embryo is conceived from human sperm and eggs is a human being.[9]

What Singer does not explain precisely is whether his functional view of personhood and how humans develop

9   Peter Singer, *Writings on an Ethical Life* (New York: HarperCollins Publishers Inc., 2000), 127.

is objectively intrinsic or merely subjective to the opinions of society.

This Substance Theory which allows room for a hyle-morphic view of humanity is rejected not because of dis-agreement over the physical empirical data concerning the embryo and her development, but because of *philo-sophical* skepticism. However, it seems that some adopt the reality of substance for pragmatic purposes in life, but this seems contradictory. As Thomas Howe said in de-fense of Aristotle:

> If there is no substance, then predication cannot make any assertion about the essence of any-thing. As Aristotle argues, "In general those who talk like this do away with substance and essence, for they are compelled to assert that all things are accidents, and that there is no such thing as 'being essentially man' or 'animal.' But if there is no substance, then words cannot have reference to what a thing essentially is. Conse-quently, words would not have a definite range of meaning, but would be unlimited in refer-ence. As Aristotle concluded, "If . . . it be said that 'man' has an infinite number of meanings, obviously there can be no discourse; for not to have one meaning is to have no meaning, and if words have no meaning, there is an end of discourse with others, and even, strictly speak-ing, with oneself. . . ." [10]

---

10 Aristotle, Metaphysics, 1007a34., cited by Howe, Thomas 1991. "Toward a Thomistic Theory of Meaning." Master's Thesis, Lib-erty University.

Perhaps David Hume is the most influential in his skepticism towards substance, so we will take a look at where his critique lies. Hume's empiricism seems to have influenced that of many contemporary naturalistic ethicists. Hume wrote:

> It is confessed by the most judicious philosophers, that our ideas of bodies are nothing but collections formed by the mind of the ideas of the several distinct sensible qualities, of which objects are composed, and which we find to have a constant union with each other. But however these qualities may in themselves be entirely distinct, it is certain we commonly regard the compound, which they form, as ONE thing, and as continuing the SAME under very considerable alterations. The acknowledged composition is evidently contrary to this supposed simplicity, and the variation to the identity. It may, therefore, be worthwhile to consider the causes, which make us almost universally fall into such evident contradictions, as well as the means by which we endeavour to conceal them.[11]

Hume continues:

> The notion of accidents is an unavoidable consequence of this method of thinking with regard to substances and substantial forms; nor can we forbear looking upon colours, sounds, tastes,

11   David Hume, *A Treatise of Human Nature,* Sect. III.

figures, and other properties of bodies, as existences, which cannot subsist apart, but require a subject of inhesion to sustain and support them. For having never discovered any of these sensible qualities, where, for the reasons abovementioned, we did not likewise fancy a substance to exist; the same habit, which makes us infer a connection betwixt cause and effect, makes us here infer a dependence of every quality on the unknown substance. The custom of imagining a dependence has the same effect as the custom of observing it would have. This conceit, however, is no more reasonable than any of the foregoing. Every quality being a distinct thing from another, may be conceived to exist apart, and may exist apart, not only from every other quality, but from that unintelligible chimera of a substance. But these philosophers carry their fictions still farther in their sentiments concerning occult qualities, and both suppose a substance supporting, which they do not understand, and an accident supported, of which they have as imperfect an idea.[12]

Hume said that it is fiction when philosophers suppose a substance existing that unites the particular qualities. In reply, let us agree that Hume is correct that the five empirical senses may not directly provide access to substance. However, Hume seems to commit a non sequitur while automatically concluding that substance cannot be known. I would ask Hume, "Why is it necessarily true

12   Ibid.

that substance is unknowable just because our initial empirical experience observes particulars?" It seems that the human senses do initially perceive only the accidents. However, if immaterial realities do exist (of which we have provided several reasons), there could be good reasons not to be dogmatic in concluding that substance is unknowable. Thomism provides another explanation in that the immaterial mind perceives the essence. The senses first perceive the empirical data such as height, size, and location, but the mind can apprehend beyond the physical impressions and know the substance of the man. Some ethicists have been influenced by Hume and therefore deny the substance or nature actually exists or is knowable. Ethicists who believe that the substance of a baby is knowable also conclude that the fetus is not an individual substance of a rational nature.

Chapter 8.

All Humans Are Persons

If the substance theory is correct, then there could be good reasons to believe that all human beings are persons. The term "First substance" refers to *individuals* like Socrates, not just generalities like the word *man*. Individuality is key to substance. Persons are individuals. George P. Klubertanz wrote, "A human being is a person by having his own act of existing."[1] To the contrary, abortion defender Michael Tooley argues that personhood is an entirely different concept and should not be united with a human being. In his book, *Abortion and Infanticide,* he said:

> One of the crucial questions involved in the issue of the morality of abortion is that of the moral significance of purely biological facts, such as the fetus's belonging to a certain species. When 'person' and 'human being' are used interchangeably, or when 'human being' is used in such a way that it either entails that something is a person, or that it has a right to life, then it is natural to suppose that belonging to a particular biological species is morally relevant—an assumption almost universally

1 George Klubertanz, *Introduction to Philosophy of Being* (New York: Meredith Publishing Company, 1963), 252.

embraced by popular anti-abortion movements, where great stress is placed upon the genetic and physiological characteristics of embryos and fetuses developing inside human mothers.[2]

Tooley, Singer, Thomson, Boonin and the majority of defenders of abortion believe strongly in a separation between human beings and personhood. This separation is to the extent that the physiological facts concerning the embryo are surpassed by the rights of the mother's autonomy. Some of these contemporary advocates of abortion, like Tooley, downplay not only the biological facts concerning the unborn babies, but also the ontological nature in general. As a result, it is not always clear when the pro-abortion ethicist is affirming an intrinsic nature of personhood that will develop in the human being with certain levels of consciousness *or* if personhood is not ontological but merely a status that society determines for certain functions.

Nevertheless, the four well-known philosophical advocates of abortion — Tooley, Singer, Thomson, and Boonin — all affirm a separation between "human being" and "person." Now to some non-philosophers this sharp separation may seem odd. After all, Webster's first definition says a person is "a human being."[3] Children do not think there is vast separation between their mother's human nature and personhood. Does not the host at the restaurant who finds a table for five human beings,

2   Michael Tooley, *Abortion and Infanticide* (New York: Oxford University Press, 1983), 61.
3   Webster's Dictionary Online "Person" retrieved at http://www.merriam-webster.com/dictionary/person.

assume that the members of homo sapiens who walked in the restaurant are *persons*? Just as with many other words that have similar but distinct usages in definitions, the word person can be used differently. So when we debate on the issue of personhood, it is important for us to understand some of the distinctions.

The word person can be used in a variety of ways in common language. First, a human, individual—sometimes used in combination especially by those who prefer to avoid *man* in compounds applicable to both sexes.[4] Second, the Latin form of the word was originally used to describe a character or mask, as in a play. Third, we can use this word to describe one of the three persons in the Trinitarian Godhead as understood by Christians. For example, Christians say that Christ is the second "person" in the Trinity. Fourth, we use the words first person, second person and third person in the grammatical way to reference the discourse to the speaker, to one spoken to, or to one spoken of as indicated by means of certain pronouns or as in some languages, the declension of the verbs. Fifth, we also use the term "in person" to describe one's bodily presence. For example, "When I was at the White House, I saw the president of the United States *in person*." Tooley and Singer reject that a "person" is the same as a human being.

In one sense, I agree with Tooley and Singer that the terms "human being" and "person" are not synonymous or necessarily interchangeable, but it does not follow that some human beings are not persons. Early medieval

---

4   This set of definitions is adapted from Webster's Dictionary Online "Person" retrieved at http://www.merriam-webster.com/dictionary/person.

Christian philosophers were the first to write extensively on the concept of "person" to apply to non-humans. God the Father was called a Person and so was the Holy Spirit. During theological conversations concerning the doctrine of the Divine, theologians were attempting to understand the Oneness of God, while maintaining a distinction in the Father, Son, and Holy Spirit. Boethius (480 AD–525 AD) defined a person as the "individual substance of a rational nature." This is the definition that I am affirming and also applying to all human beings, including the unborn. Robert Spaemann explains the importance of this definition:

> What does it mean to say that rational natures exist as persons? Of course, 'person' here is a *nomen dignitatis*; rational natures command a definite kind of respect. But the primary sense of Boethius's definition is ontological: the *natura rationalis* exists as being-in-itself. But that is to say that an individual existing in this way cannot be displayed in full by any possible description. No description can replace *naming*. A person is someone, not something, not a mere instance of a kind of being that is indifferent to it.[5]

Spaemann observes that Boethius's definition is ontological, not something that society determines based on a set of functions. Boethius's idea of personhood is related to an intrinsic individuality that is valuable because of his or

5   Robert Spaemann, *Persons* (Oxford: Oxford University Press, 1996), 29.

her being-in-itself, not for the value it contributes to the society. It is essential to Boethius that there is a *unity* between nature and individual substance. Being a member of the human race and being a person is *distinct* but not *separate*. Robert Spitzer wrote:

> The linguistic evidence shows that throughout history, the word "person" has had a primarily ontological meaning, which defines words according to the nature of things, that is, what a thing is. Thus, "person" was inseparable from "a living individual human being." If the majority (in Roe v. Wade) had made recourse to the linguistic history of "person" (and had, thereby, become acquainted with the ontological meaning of "person," a human being) before seeking a legal definition of it from case precedents it would not have separated "person" from "human being" and would have presumed that the human fetus is a person because human fetuses are genetically distinct human organisms, rather than parts of human organism.[6]

Spitzer is correct that being a human "person" and being a "human being" are inseparable ontologically. In everyday language, this is how we understand that people are someone because of who they are, namely, that they have the nature of human beings. Every single human being from embryo to natural death is an individual substance of a rational nature. But not only are they individual, they

6   Robert Spitzer, *Ten Universal Principles* (San Francisco: Ignatius Press, 2011), 28.

are *supposits* in the sense that they have their own proper act of existing.

George Klubertanz explained:

> The term "subsistent" is used to mean "something which exists with its own proper and proportionate act of existing." What then is the difference between an individual thing and a supposit? But the term "individual thing" only connotes an act of existing, while the term "supposit" explicitly means having its own proper act of existing. A technical term sometimes used for "supposit" is the word "hypostasis." The supposit in a rational nature has a special term, namely "person." A person, therefore, from the point of view of metaphysics, is a "rational supposit," that is, a "distinct subsistent individual in a rational nature." Personality, therefore, namely that (quasi form) by which a person is precisely a person, is the proper act of existing proportioned to a rational nature. In other words, a human being is a person by having his own act of existing.[7]

Human beings by individuality indicate the act of existing. Each embryo *is*. The word *hypostasis* mentioned by Klubertanz could mean *beneath-standing* or *underpinning* and *the existence* of some thing. Their rational nature is inherent as each person exists from conception, even though the *manifestation* of personality may be discovered later; regardless, the unity of person and nature of homo sapiens

7   Klubertanz, 252.

is unbreakable from conception until natural death. Those who hold to abortion defense will therefore affirm that personhood is not only distinct, but *completely separate* from biological nature. Therefore some, like Singer, who hold the functional view of personhood will argue that if a non-human animal like a dolphin or a dog is smart, then they achieve "personhood," while certain human races, along with infants and elderly people are denied personhood. However, the pro-abortionist is inconsistent to later make some claims of "personhood." Peter Singer and Thomson have declared that they are not moral relativists. Singer admits that relativism is self-defeating. He writes, "The fourth, and last, claim about ethics that I shall deny in the chapter is that ethics is relative or subjective."[8] But it is uncertain on what *ontological basis* Singer can declare that personhood objectively exists. If their naturalistic foundations are correct, then how can Singer and others claim objectively that personhood is based on self-awareness, self-control, and a sense of the future?

If personhood is not applied to the weakest of human beings including newborn babies, the elderly, and the handicapped, then Singer does not seem consistent in his book and website, *The Life You Can Save*, which say we should help those who are dying in poverty and disease. For Singer to be consistent, he must admit that many of the dying that we can save have lost some capacities of self-control or awareness of the future. Singer wrote:

> For the first time in history, it is now within
> our reach to eradicate world poverty and the

8   Peter Singer, *Writings on an Ethical Life* (New York: HarperCollins Publishers Inc., 2000), 9.

suffering it brings. . . . And though the number of deaths attributable to poverty worldwide has fallen dramatically in the past half-century, nearly nine million children still die unnecessarily each year. The people of the developed world face a profound choice: If we are not to turn our backs on a fifth of the world's population, we must become part of the solution.[9]

Singer's recent project *The Life You Can Save* has an end goal of reaching those who are dying and suffering in third world countries. However, if lesser functioning people are not really persons, Singer lacks the ontological case for the dignity of those human beings. We should be concerned, but on what basis is he going to grant personhood?

Singer's utilitarianism and functional view of personhood applied to only the healthiest and smartest humans seems similar to that of Margaret Sanger, the founder of Planned Parenthood in Brooklyn, New York. In her book *Woman, Morality and Birth Control,* published in New York in 1922, Sanger said, "Birth control must lead ultimately to a cleaner race."[10] "Her [Sanger's] mother had 18 pregnancies, bore 11 children, and died in 1899 at the age of 40. Working as a nurse with immigrant families on New York's Lower East Side, Sanger witnessed the sickness, misery, and death that resulted from unwanted pregnancy

9 Peter Singer, *The Life You Can Save* (New York: Random House, 2009).
10 Margaret Sanger, *Woman, Morality, and Birth Control* (New York: New York Publishing Company, 1922), 12.

and illegal abortion."[11] In her article, "A Plan for Peace," Sanger wrote, "Keep the doors of immigration closed to the entrance of certain aliens whose condition is known to be detrimental to the stamina of the race."[12] She added, "Apply a stern and rigid policy of sterilization and segregation to that grade of population whose progeny (i.e. offspring) is already tainted."[13] Sanger also believed that the world's population was growing too fast and that having too many children could also put a strain on well-educated white families as well. In her book, *Woman and the New Race*, Sanger wrote, "THE most serious evil of our times is that of encouraging the bringing into the world of large families. The most immoral practice of the day is breeding too many children."[14]

If personhood is something that society determines based on functions, one cannot make a case to rescue those who are suffering. Peter Singer said, "My suggestion, then, is that we accord the life of a fetus no greater value than the life of a nonhuman animal at a similar level of rationality, self-consciousness, awareness, capacity to feel, etc."[15] Personhood according to Boethius was intrinsic, not something that law or society gives. The functional view of personhood that Sanger, Singer, and Tooley all subscribe to shares some similarities to ancient Roman

11 Planned Parenthood, "History and Successes" retrieved at http://www.plannedparenthood.org/about-us/who-we-are/history-and-successes.htm#Sanger.

12 Margaret Sanger, "Plan for Peace" in *Birth Control Review* (April 1932), 107–8.

13 Ibid.

14 Margaret Sanger, *Woman and the New Race* (New York: Truth Publishing Company, 1920), 58. (Emphasis in the original.)

15 Singer, *Practical Ethics*, second ed. (Cambridge: Cambridge University Press, 1993), 151.

philosophy in which slaves did not have the legal rights of personhood. In others, personhood is something that society determines. It also seems that contemporary pro-abortionists have misused the classical definition "individual substance of a rational nature" while rejecting the classical notion of "substance" and assuming the usage of "nature" in the modern sense to mean physical laws of nature. The ruling on the Roe v. Wade case declared:

> The appellee and certain amici argue that the fetus is a "person" within the language and meaning of the Fourteenth Amendment. In support of this, they outline at length and in detail the well-known facts of fetal development. If this suggestion of personhood is established, the appellant's case, of course, collapses, for the fetus' right to life would then be guaranteed specifically by the Amendment. The appellant conceded as much on re-argument. On the other hand, the appellee conceded on re-argument that no case could be cited that holds that a fetus is a person within the meaning of the Fourteenth Amendment.[16]

Robert Spitzer gives an analysis of this declaration:

> So what criterion did the majority use to try to establish the presence of personhood, when it did not use the criterion of "a being of human origin with a full human genome"? Remarkably, it searched for a previous case that

---

16   Roe v. Wade, Supreme Court Decision, Section IX.

acknowledges that a fetus was a person, and when it could not find one, it assumed that fetuses were not persons. This criterion is not sufficient to sanction a violation of the principle of nonmaleficence, because "personhood" is not merely a legal concept; it is essentially an ontological concept (i.e. it defines what a being is, namely, human) and an ethical concept (i.e. it defines the kind of being that we are obligated not to kill, abuse, or harm unnecessarily because of its intrinsic worth as human).[17]

The word *fetus* was a Latin word that meant offspring. Originally it could be used interchangeably with the offspring who were already born as well as well as offspring in the womb. Similarly, the ancient and koine Greek word *brephos* was used to described babies inside the womb and outside the womb. However, during Roe v. Wade, the Court could not find that a fetus was defined as a person, so they made up a definition as legal concept. But Spitzer is correct in pointing out that "personhood" is not merely a legal concept that society determines, but is ontological reality.

17 Robert Spitzer, *Ten Universal Principles* (San Francisco: Ignatius Press, 2011), 26–27.

}92{

Chapter 9.

All Human Persons Are Someone for Who They Are and Not Someone for What They Do

We are first human *beings* before we are human *doings*. Human persons by nature are both physical and nonphysical. Human persons are different from inanimate physical objects. We are animate objects composed of body and soul. The immaterial aspect of humanity provides the best explanation of why human persons are free to choose and are not merely determined by their matter. Thomas Aquinas stated, "The human soul, which is called the intellect of the mind, is something incorporeal and subsistent."[1] A philosophical defense of hylomorphism, which was originated with Aristotle and was later developed by Aquinas, conceived "being" as a compound of matter and form. The word "hylomorphism," is a nineteenth-century term formed from the Greek words ὕλη-hyle, "wood, matter," and μορφή, "form."[2] This concept is best understood in the context of Aristotle's understanding of causality: efficient, final, formal, and material causality.[3] Modern naturalistic philosophers have dis-

---

1   Thomas Aquinas, *Summa* I.75.2
2   Hylomorphism definition adapted from Aristotle.
3   "A heart, for example, cannot be understood except as being an organ having a certain material constitution (its material cause), as possessing a certain form or principle of organization (its formal

missed final and formal causality, which denote purpose and nature. Edward Feser wrote:

> Materialism and Cartesian dualism alike eliminate formal and final causes from the explanation of material things, replacing the classical hylomorphic conception of matter substances as inherently purposive composites of matter and form with a conception of them as collections of particles or the like devoid of either intrinsic purpose or objective, irreducible form, and explicable entirely in terms of efficient causation.[4]

Feser suggests that hylomorphic dualism gives the best explanation for the identity problem. Again, Feser means hylomorphism in the view that

> [A] concrete substance is a composite of matter and form. The form of a substance is its organizational structure; the matter is that which is given organizational structure by the form. Substantial form is that specific aspect of a substance's organizational structure by virtue of which it is the kind of substance it is.[5]

cause), as serving a certain function—to pump blood (its final cause)—and as having been brought about by antecedents such as the genetic programming inherent in certain cells that led them to develop into a heart rather than a kidney or liver (its efficient cause)." Edward Feser, *Philosophy of Mind* (Oxford: One World Publishing, 2006), 221.

4   Edward Feser, *Philosophy of Mind* (Oxford: One World Publishing, 2006), 221.
5   Ibid.

Earlier, we mentioned that abortion defender David Boonin had several pictures of his son Eli, including a sonogram that he was convinced was the same boy. But what is it that makes a person throughout this whole experience of change? René Descartes believed in his dualism that the body changes, but the real person who remains is the *res cogitans*, which he identified as a mind. But contrary to Descartes, hylomorphism says that beings are a compound of matter and form. Feser responds to the Cartesian view, "Given that all I can ever observe is your bodily characteristics and behavior, how do I know they are associated with a mind? How do I know you're not a zombie?"[6] Francis Beckwith says that personhood is not linked to a functioning, but rather that it is the underlying *unity* of the individual. Beckwith states:

> What is crucial morally is the being of a person, not his or her functioning. A human person does not come into existence when human function arises, but rather, a human person is an entity who has the natural inherent capacity to give rise to human functions, whether or not those functions are ever attained. . . . A human person who lacks the ability to think rationally (either because she is too young or she suffers from a disability) is still a human person because of her nature. Consequently, it makes sense to speak of a human being's lack if and only if she is an actual person.[7]

6   Ibid., 213.
7   Francis J. Beckwith, "Abortion, Bioethics, and Personhood: A Philosophical Reflection," The Southern Baptist Journal of Theology, Spring 2000.vol 4.1, p. 20.

Beings do not come into existence because of certain functions, rather they maintain a unity, even if functions are not working properly. A Presbyterian minister in my city once said that he would support his teenage daughter to get an abortion. When another pastor asked him, "When do you believe a human person begins to exist?" The Presbyterian minister replied, "I think someone becomes a person when they are loved." This answer is quite revealing. Right now, there many children outside the womb who are sick and unloved. Are they still persons? W. Norris Clarke refutes the idea that relationship and responding to relationship is one of the determining functions for personhood. He wrote:

> Metaphysically this will not work. We cannot literally bring into being another person that was not there before simply by relating to the thing that is there with attentive love. Try doing this with a rock, a tree, or a rattlesnake! The being to which we relate must already be the type that can respond to an invitation by intrinsic powers already within it.[8]

Persons certainly do have the intrinsic power to perform functions like responding in love, but if these functions do not work properly, they still maintain personhood. Persons do have certain capacities that may be manifested at different times. However, persons maintain a unity even though they change. Human beings are exceptional because of the kind of being they are. Since we have good

8   W. Norris Clarke, S.J., *Person and Being*, (Milwaukee: Marquette University Press, 2004), 58–59.

reasons not to reject the substance view, one can make a case for believing in human exceptionalism. Francis Beckwith wrote:

> According to the substance view, a human being is intrinsically valuable because of the sort of thing it is and the human being remains that sort of thing as long as it exists. What sort of thing is it? The human being is a particular type of substance — a rational moral agent — that remains identical to itself as long as it exists, even if it is not presently exhibiting the functions, behaving in ways, or currently able to immediately exercise these activities that we typically attribute to active and mature rational moral agents.[9]

When Francis Beckwith said that a human being is intrinsically valuable, Beckwith is using the word *value* in an objective sense, not in a subjective sense, because of what society feels about the individual human being. Abortion defenders frequently reject this notion of "value" toward humans. Mary Anne Warren says,

> Opponents of abortion will reply that abortion is wrong, not simply because fetuses are *alive,* but because they are *human.* But why should we believe that the destruction of a living human organism is always morally worse than the destruction of an organism of some other species?

9 Francis Beckwith, *Defending Life* (Cambridge, Cambridge University Press, 2007), 132.

> Membership in a particular biological species does not appear to be, in itself, any more relevant to moral status than membership in a particular race or sex.[10]

In reply, if there is no such thing as a substance or human sanctity and we are merely cells, then Warren is correct and there is nothing morally different from chopping down trees or chopping down your newborn. However, the human mind has the capacity to apprehend not just physical cells but an actual person. Peter Singer said,

> The only thing that distinguishes the infant from the animal, in the eyes of those who claim it has a "right to life," is that it is, biologically, a member of the species homo sapiens, whereas chimpanzees, dogs, and pigs are not. But to use this difference as the basis for granting a right to life to the infant and not to the other animals is, of course, pure "speciesism."[11]

Singer adds:

> The argument could be taken both ways. Alternatively one could take the argument as showing that the severely retarded and hopelessly senile have no right to life and may be killed for quite trivial reasons, as we now kill animals.[12]

---

10 Singer, *A Companion to Ethics*, 308.
11 Ibid., 44.
12 Ibid.

Some advocates of abortion (e.g., Warren and Singer) have popularized the term "speciesism" as a derogatory term designating humans who believe that humans are morally superior to other animals. However, even those who favor the elevation of animal rights apprehend a higher level of responsibility for a human being. Scott Klusendorf said:

> Radical animal rights activists are mistaken. A robust belief in human exceptionalism does not exploit animals; it protects them from unjust harm. Consider the case of suspended (NFL) quarterback Michael Vick, sentenced to jail for dog fighting and gratuitous cruelty to animals. According to one report, "the 52 pit bulls found on Vick's estate were mostly emaciated" and kept "ravenously hungry so that they would eagerly assail the flesh of the dogs they met in the ring." The losing animals, the reporter said, "were sometimes executed if they didn't die in the fight. One dog, the grand jury reported, was hosed down after a loss and then electrocuted." When a raging Michael Vick clubs his pit bull to death for losing a fight, we're justifiably outraged at his inhumane and beastly behavior. But why are we outraged? Isn't it because we demand better of him *as a man*? Our revulsion of Vick makes no sense unless humans are exceptional. After all, prosecutors and critics are not blaming the dogs in this case; they are blaming humans who ought to behave better than animals. When dogs or rhinos tear each other up or kill unsuspecting prey, there's a reason we don't slap them with jail time. They don't have

consciences, and they don't know better. They're just doing what comes naturally. If you keep telling humans they are no different than animals, don't be surprised when they act that way.[13]

Even abortion defenders recognize that Vick was guilty for acting in a way that was inhumane. We certainly don't apply this high standard to animals. Maybe with our own pets we have high standards, but what about other animals in the wild? Although morally Michael Vick did some very bad things, he is still ontologically a man and is expected to act better. Humans deserve respect and accountability because of the type of being they are. They shouldn't act like animals. Human babies are innocent. They are persons and human, therefore they should be protected and should not be intentionally killed.

13 Scott Klusendorf, *The Case for Life* (Wheaton: Crossway, 2009), 56–57.

Chapter 10.

Conclusion: Similarities and Differences

It may seem very difficult for a philosopher of religion to share areas of agreement with someone like Peter Singer who supports human infanticide, bestiality, and incest. It does seem inconsistent that an ethicist teaching at *Center of Human Value* openly respects some animals more than some human babies and the elderly. I certainly have disagreements with Peter Singer and other defenders of abortion choice. While there are fundamental differences, there are also some areas of ethics held by Singer and other abortion choice advocates that a non-atheist philosopher and even a Christian can also affirm. I will first share some areas of similarity and then some areas of disagreement.

There can be a greater purpose in some suffering

Peter Singer is a strong believer that suffering is bad, but he does admit that some pain is justified because it leads to less suffering. Singer admits, "We do this ourselves when we go to the dentist and we do it to others when we reprimand a child or jail a criminal."[1] Many who hold to theism (Judaism and Christianity) will say that God permits certain evils, sufferings and natural disasters. Our temporary lives on earth are affected by wills that are evil,

---

1   Peter Singer, *Writings on an Ethical Life* (New York: HarperCollins Publishers Inc., 2000), xv.

sinful actions and laws of nature that can result in death. God does not always intervene to stop evil people or the laws of nature that cause suffering. Christians believe God allows his creatures to experience such sufferings and evils for some end (which we may not fully comprehend) while holding to a future hope of a resurrected body and the promise that God will eventually defeat evil.

Humans are responsible for what they could have prevented.

One of Peter Singer's foundations is that humans are responsible for not only what they do but also what we could have prevented. His fourth foundation says,

> We would never kill a stranger, but we know that our intervention will save the lives of many strangers in a distant country, and yet do nothing. We do not then think of ourselves in a way responsible for the deaths of these strangers. This is a mistake.[2]

There is some truth to this. There are sins of commission but also sins of omission. The apostle James wrote:

> If a brother or sister is without clothing and in need of daily food, and one of you says to them, "Go in peace, be warmed and be filled," and yet you do not give them what is necessary for *their* body, what use is that? Anyone who knows the right thing to do, but does not do it, is sinning. (James 2:15–17)

2   Ibid., xvi.

There also seem to be similarities between of a variety of religious and philosophical beliefs, recognizing a golden rule, or moral principles, such as . . .

Racism is wrong.

Singer for the most part implies that racism amongst human beings is wrong. Singer mentions Thomas Jefferson, appealing to the equality of men in the American Declaration. Jefferson theoretically opposed slavery and believed it was wrong, but he was hypocritical in his behavior and owned slaves. Jefferson emphasized the intellectual achievements of the black children and refuted the idea that they had limited intellectual capacities. Both Singer and pro-life ethicists will affirm much of Jefferson's belief of opposing slavery, while also disagreeing with Jefferson's hypocritical actions of owning slaves. Both pro-abortion and pro-life philosophers argue that racism is morally wrong.

Animals should be treated with respect.

Although I disagree with Singer giving animals equal value with some humans, he is correct when he says that animals should be treated with respect. Although Singer claims that the Bible is the key influential work of literature that is anti-animal, it is not. The Bible teaches that animals should be taken care of. Proverbs 12:10 says, "Good people take care of their animals." God declared animals "good" in Genesis. Jesus said, "Five sparrows are sold for only two pennies, and God does not forget any of them." Has Peter Singer forgotten about any sparrows? Of course, we all have, but Christian doctrine says God does not forget any of them.

A fetus is an individual member of the species "homo sapiens."

While some abortion advocates have argued that the fetus is an extension of the mother's womb, Singer does not do this. He admits, "Whether a being is a member of a given species is something that can be determined scientifically, by an examination of the nature of the chromosomes in the cells of the living organisms. In this sense there is no doubt that from the first moments of its existence an embryo conceived from human sperm and eggs is a human being."[3] He also adds, "The human embryo, fetus and disabled child are a member of homo sapiens."[4]

There are a few minor aspects of ethical thought that we can affirm from Peter Singer and other ethicists who hold views similar to his. For pragmatic conversational purposes, if we are in a dialogue with someone who holds Singer's philosophy, we could begin by saying that we actually have some areas of common ground. We can affirm that there can be a greater purpose in some suffering, that animals should be treated with respect, that a fetus is a member of homo sapiens species, and that all ethics cannot be relative. After beginning with one of these similarities, we could then challenge the differences.

Philosophers' ethical stance of abortion is frequently rooted in their metaphysical beliefs.

One of the key differences that I discussed earlier was the ontological, intrinsic unity between personhood and being a member of homo sapiens. Singer has affirmed that the fetus in the womb of a female human is an individual

3   Ibid., 127.
4   Ibid.

member of the species homo sapiens, but he then created a separation from personhood. Singer said,

> the indicators of humanhood include: self-awareness, self-control, and a sense of the future, a sense of the past, the capacity to relate to others.[5]

He continued:

> The human embryo, fetus and disabled child are a member of "homo sapiens," but none are self-aware, have a sense of the future, or have the capacity to relate to others. Therefore a disabled child is not human.[6]

Singer believed that *personhood* and being human is not united with the child. He does not provide adequate philosophical reasoning that disabilities in children strip homo sapiens of value. Norman Geisler wrote, "Abortion of the handicapped is not promoted by handicapped people. At last count, there was not a single organization for parents of handicapped children on record as favoring abortion of the handicapped."[7] From experience, we know friends who have had children with Down syndrome, severe autism or Spina Bifida. Raising such children is not going to be easy. Some of these women were encouraged by their physicians to have an abortion. But today, every

5   Ibid., 127.
6   Ibid.
7   Norman L. Geisler, *Christian Ethics, Options and Issues* (Grand Rapids: Baker Books, 1989), 141.

one of those parents will say that they are thankful that they chose life for their child.[8] Singer who denies the personhood of handicapped children is also not clear on how personhood is maintained when certain functions are not being manifested with "normal" human beings. What about when normal persons encounter deep sleep, slip into a coma, or are under sedation? Under such circumstances, there is always the possibility that the person may not wake up. Many times they wake, but other times they do not. According to Singer's own standards, how could a non-person (a baby inside the womb) become a person (while they are a toddler)? And then how could that same person become a non-person (going into a coma after a wreck), but then become a person again (coming out of the coma some weeks later)?

Mark Foreman wrote, "In order for a being to do something it has to exist. Existence must always precede action. In relation to personhood, a person must already

8   Singer observes that many parents want to abort their handicapped children, but from experience there are many examples of ordinary parents who see their children with Down syndrome as true persons. For example, a mother named Annie Reid wrote a blog post this morning, speaking about her three-year old daughter Ollie, who has Down syndrome. She said, "I have learned there is beauty in 'imperfections.' I don't believe Ollie is one bit imperfect but in the eyes of many she is. There is great beauty in all her God given pieces. Her crooked pinky fingers, the light spots in her eyes, the way she smiles. . . . Her tiny little heart, a heart beat that doesn't beat quite as it should but it's healthy — oh that heart beat is precious." This mom, like other moms who have three-year-old children with Down syndrome, are very thankful for their sons and daughters, and thankful that they chose life. Annie Reid, "What to Expect if Your Baby Has Down Syndrome" *The House That Jade Built*, http://networkedblogs.com/WekvO retrieved on April 23, 2014.

exist in order to function as one. It is not the functioning that *makes* one a person, she already is a person— that is why she functioning that way. It is *being* a person that grants one the capacity to *function* as a person."[9] In contrast to Singer and other defenders of abortion, I believe there is a fundamental difference between *being* and *doing*. We are human *beings*. A person exists, and then the functions follow.

Those in favor of abortion frequently emphasize hypotheticals, while defenders of life use Aristotelean logic with premises about real life.

During the research and writing phases of this thesis, a key difference between abortion advocates (including Singer, Thomson and Boonin) and abortion opponents (including Beckwith, Kaczor, Spitzer and Kreeft) became evident. The difference was the way these philosophers made use of logic and hypotheticals. It seemed that many philosophers who argued for abortion rights emphasized hypotheticals that frequently favored analogies and symbols that spoke of possibilities and probabilities. Many of those who argued against abortion favor classical Aristotelian logic which uses real words that correspond to reality. Peter Kreeft provided a helpful comparison:

> Symbolic logic is essentially a logic, "if . . . then . . . ," a logic of antecedent and consequent propositions; and it is mathematical logic, a logic of quantity. These two features perfectly fit and foster utilitarianism in ethics because

9   Mark Foreman, *Christianity and Bioethics* (New York: College Press Publishing, 1999), 82.

utilitarianism is essentially an ethics of "if . . . then . . . ," an ethics of consequences, and it is also an ethics of quantity. For its fundamental principle is that an act is ethically good if its foreseeable consequences constitute, "the greatest happiness for the greatest number." . . . In contrast, Aristotelian logic naturally fits and fosters a natural-law ethics because its basic unit is a term that expresses a nature or essence, and its basic judgment is "all S is P," which is a statement of universal truth or law about the nature or quality of S (as expressed in P). . . . Symbolic logic has no way of knowing, and prevents us from saying, *what* anything is! But that was the essential Socratic question about everything."[10]

Although there are some helpful aspects of shorthand with symbolic logic as well as clearness, sometimes the hypotheticals, though coherent, miss what is real. Abortion choice defenders would often combine the use of hypothetical syllogisms, by dismissing the *existence* of the first premise and then provide an analogy of a story containing a moral dilemma. Then the abortion defender challenged the pro-life defender to respond to this unusual scenario. But these analogies frequently do not exist in real life. Perhaps no hypothetical that defends abortion is cited or adapted from as much as Thomson's violin analogy. Although this is a long citation for a conclusion, I think it is necessary for understanding. She wrote:

10 Peter Kreeft, "Clashing Symbols," *Touchstone* (November, December 2012), 39.

I propose, then, that we grant that the fetus is a person from the moment of conception. How does the argument go from here? Something like this, I take it. Every person has a right to life. So the fetus has a right to life. No doubt the mother has a right to decide what shall happen in and to her body; everyone would grant that. But surely a person's right to life is stronger and more stringent than the mother's right to decide what happens in and to her body, and so outweighs it. So the fetus may not be killed; an abortion may not be performed.

It sounds plausible. But now let me ask you to imagine this. You wake up in the morning and find yourself back to back in bed with an unconscious violinist. A famous unconscious violinist. He has been found to have a fatal kidney ailment, and the Society of Music Lovers has canvassed all the available medical records and found that you alone have the right blood type to help. They have therefore kidnapped you, and last night the violinist's circulatory system was plugged into yours, so that your kidneys can be used to extract poisons from his blood as well as your own. The director of the hospital now tells you, "Look, we're sorry the Society of Music Lovers did this to you—we would never have permitted it if we had known. But still, they did it, and the violinist is now plugged into you. To unplug you would be to kill him. But never mind, it's only for nine months. By then he will have recovered from his ailment, and can safely be unplugged from you." Is it

morally incumbent on you to accede to this sit-
uation? No doubt it would be very nice of you
if you did, a great kindness. But do you have to
accede to it? What if it were not nine months,
but nine years? Or longer still? What if the director of the hospital says, "Tough luck. I agree.
But now you've got to stay in bed, with the violinist plugged into you, for the rest of your
life."[11]

After this story, she then explained how this analogy com-
pares to abortion. There are many problems with this
analogy. Although she proposes that a fetus is a person at
the moment of conception, she does not deal with the ethical implications of this *reality*. It seems that this *existence*
of the person does not matter as much to Thompson as
the fictional violin story that follows. Second, she provided a hypothetical story that, while quite interesting,
did not correspond with an actual baby and a baby's
mother.

But one might wonder how her long story connected
with logic and the use of hypotheticals? Again Peter
Kreeft is helpful in explaining how logic is related to *everything*. Kreeft said,

Logic and social change are not unrelated.
(Logic is not unrelated to *anything*.) Our society no longer thinks about the fundamental
metaphysical question, the question of *what*
something is, the question of the "nature" of a

11   Judith Jarvis Thomson, *Rights, Restitution & Risk* (Cambridge: Harvard University Press, 1986), 1.

thing. Instead, we think about how we feel about things, how we can use them, how they work.[12]

Someone's misuse of a hypothetical combined with a denial of metaphysical and epistemological realism will often lead one to argue by creating fictional dilemmas. So in Thomson's analogy, even though she grants the full personhood of the unborn baby, it is irrelevant because she is downplaying the "whatness" and "existence" of the actual nature of the baby. There is a problem with the famous violinist who is depending on you and your blood alone. The violinist, who has been attached to you in your sleep because you alone have their blood type, *does not exist*. The analogy misunderstands the natural purpose of sexuality and reproduction and ignores the personhood of the actual baby. Over 99% of pregnancies are not the result of rape but are the result of sexual relations in a consensual relationship. Human sexuality flourishes best in the context of a monogamous relationship between husband and wife. Through misrepresenting the beauty of the true nature of marriage and motherhood, the violin analogy creates a false dichotomy in which the mother and child are strangers and set against each other as enemies. Randy Alcorn critiques Thomson's analogy, "The mother is at best merely a life-support system and at worst the victim of crime . . . the bonding between mother and child is totally ignored. The picture of a woman waking up in a bed, strapped to a strange unconscious man is bizarre and degrading to women, whose pregnancy and motherhood

12 Peter Kreeft, "Clashing Symbols," *Touchstone* (November, December 2012), 40.

are natural."[13] Aristotelian metaphysical realities like "relation" and "substance" are ignored in these unnatural and unreal stories. Through symbolic logic combined with hypothetical syllogisms, the abortion advocate chooses an imaginary story over the reality of babies in the actual world. Again from Peter Kreeft:

> The bottom line for logic is that, if you agree with either Hume or Kant, logic becomes the mere manipulation of our symbols, not the principles for a true and orderly knowledge of an ordered world. Categories like "relation" and "quality" and "Substance," and perhaps even "time" and "self" and "God," are not real features of the world we discover, only mental classifications we make.[14]

One of Aristotle's categories that Kreeft mentioned categories was *time*. The category of time asks the questions, "When?" and "How long?" The violinist analogy depicts one being unwantedly tied to this violinist for not only nine months, but nine years and even one's entire life! But, that does not seem fair to real pregnant women. Abortionists will not perform a surgical abortion until after about six-seven weeks, because he wants to account for all the body parts of the baby within the mother's womb. If not removed, a piece of the tiny baby could cause a serious infection. Randy Alcorn wrote in repose to Thomson:

13 Randy Alcorn, *ProLife Answers to ProChoice Arguments* (Sisters, Oregon: Multnomah, 2000), 108.
14 Peter Kreeft, "Clashing Symbols," *Touchstone* (November, December 2012), 38.

Since the great majority of abortions take place from seven weeks to six months of development, the actual difference between the woman who aborts her child and the woman who doesn't is not nine months but three to seven months. The analogy to nine years or even a lifetime of being chained to someone is obviously invalid since after birth a woman is free to give up her child to one of the hundreds of thousands of families waiting to adopt infants from this country. While pregnancy is a temporary condition, abortion produces a permanent condition—the death of the child."[15]

Other categories in Aristotelian logic that are misrepresented in Thomson's analogies include "position," "state," "action," and "passivity." Pregnancy is pictured by the violin story as being really unnatural, horrific, as being tied down, bed-ridden, attached to a grown adult stranger like a bad horror movie. During most pregnancies, women live normal happy lives, enjoying interaction with family and friends, working, taking trips, going to the gym, walking in the park and going out to eat. Women certainly have times of sickness or inconvenience but these women are active, moving and living life.

Today, it seems that metaphysical truths like essence and existence are rejected, while defenders of abortion have preferred a functional view of what it means to be human. Pregnancy is often viewed negatively and children are treated like inhumane parasites. Many

15 Randy Alcorn, *ProLife Answers to ProChoice Arguments*, (Sisters, Oregon: Multnomah, 2000), 108.

contemporary defenders of abortion choice have rejected much of Aristotle's metaphysics and the scholasticism of the middle ages. Aristotle along with other of scholastics in the Middle Ages, including Thomas Aquinas, affirmed epistemological realism and metaphysical realism. We must be brought back to the Aristotelian scholastic philosophical tradition combined with the notion that human beings are contingent upon the existence of the Necessary Being, who is the Natural Law Giver and Creator of human existence. These classical truths could help progressive ethicists who are blinded by an incoherent naturalistic worldview, become more open-minded about the dignity and personhood of unborn human beings.

Bibliography

Aristotle. *Metaphysics,* trans. by W. D. Ross, retrieved http://classics.mit.edu/Aristotle/metaphysics.htm

_____. *Nicomachean Ethics.* trans. by W. D. Ross, retrieved http://classics.mit.edu/Aristotle/metaphysics.html

_____. *Physics.* trans. by W. D. Ross, retrieved http://classics.mit.edu/Aristotle/metaphysics.htm

Aquinas, Thomas. *Summa of the Summa,* edited by Peter Kreeft. San Francisco: Ignatius Press, 1990.

Ayer, A. J. *Language, Truth, and Logic.* New York: Dover Publications, 1952.

Baird, Robert M., and Stuart E. Rosenbaum. *The Ethics of Abortion,* revised edition. Buffalo: Prometheus Books, 1993.

Beckwith, Francis J. "Abortion, Bioethics, and Personhood: A Philosophical Reflection," *The Southern Baptist Theological Seminary,* retrieved online pdf.

Beckwith, Francis J. *Defending Life.* Cambridge: Cambridge University Press, 2007.

Boonin, David. *A Defense of Abortion.* Cambridge: Cambridge University Press, 2003.

Craig, William Lane. *On Guard*. Colorado Springs: David C Cook, 2010.

Craig, William Lane, and J. P. Moreland. *The Blackwell Companion to Natural Theology*. Oxford: Blackwell Publishing, 2009.

Daniel Dennett. *Breaking the Spell: Religion as a Natural Phenomenon*. New York: Viking, 2006.

Feser, Edward. *Philosophy of Mind*. Oxford: One World Publishing, 2006.

_____. *The Last Superstition*. South Bend: St. Augustine's Press, 2008.

Geisler, Norman. *Baker Encyclopedia of Christian Apologetics*. Grand Rapids: Baker, 1999.

George, P. Robert, and Christopher Tollefsen. *Embryo: A Defense of Human Life*. New York: Doubleday, 2007.

Harman, Gilbert, and Judith Thomson. *Moral Relativism and Moral Objectivity*. Oxford: Wiley-Blackwell,1996.

Hawking, Stephen, and Leonard Mlodinow. *The Grand Design*. New York: Random House, 2010.

Hilgers, Thomas W., and Dennis J. Horan. *Abortion and Social Justice*. New York: Sheed & Ward, 1972.

Hume, David. *A Treatise of Human Nature*, trans. by Lewis Amherst Selby-Bigge *1896*. retrieved *http://oll.liberty-fund.org/titles/hume-a-treatise-of-human-nature*

_____. *Letter to Stewart*. Hume Studies Volume 1, retrieved at http://www.humesociety.org/

Johnson, Philip. *The Right Questions*. Downers Grove: InterVarsity Press, 2002.

Kaczor, Christopher. *The Ethics of Abortion*. New York: Routledge, 2011.

Klunsendorf, Scott. *The Case for Life*. Wheaton: Crossway, 2009.

Kreeft, Peter. *The Unaborted Socrates*. Downers Grove: Intervarsity Press, 1983.

_____. *Three Approaches to Abortion*. San Francisco: Ignatius Press, 2002.

Lawhead, William F. *The Voyage of Discovery*. Belmont: Wadsworth/Thomson, 2002.

Lee, Patrick. *Abortion and Unborn Human Life*. Washington, D.C.: The Catholic University of America Press, 1996.

Moore, Keith. *Essentials of Human Embryology*. Toronto: BC Decker Inc, 1988.

Moreland, J. P. *The Recalcitrant Imago Dei*. London: SCM Press, 2009.

Nagel, Thomas. *Mind and Cosmos: Why the Materialist Neo-Darwinian Conception of Nature is Almost Certainly False*. Oxford: Oxford Scholarship Online, 2013.

Nathanson, Bernard N., M.D. *Abortion America*. New York: Pinnacle Books, 1981.

Plantinga, Alvin, *Where the Conflict Really Lies: Science, Religion and Naturalism*. New York: Oxford University Press, 2011.

Simmons, Paul, D. Religious Liberty and Abortion Policy: Casey as "Catch 22", Journal of Church and State 42.1 (Winter 2000): 69-88.

Singer, Peter. *Practical Ethics,* second ed. Cambridge: Cambridge University Press, 1993.

_____. *Unsanctifying Human Life*. ed. Helga Kuhse, Oxford: Blackwell Publishers, 2002.

_____. *The Life You Can Save*. New York: Random House, 2009.

_____. *Writings on an Ethical Life*. New York: HarperCollins Publishers Inc., 2000.

Spaemann, Robert. *Essays in Anthropology*. Eugene: Cascade Books, 2010.

_____. *Love and The Dignity of Human Life*. Grand Rapids: Wm. B. Eerdmans Publishing Co., 2012.

_____. *Persons: The Difference Between "Something" and "Something"*. New York: Oxford University Press, 2006.

Spitzer, Robert J. *Ten Universal Principles*. San Francisco: Ignatius Press, 2011.

Taylor, Charles. "The Concept of a Person", *Philosophical Papers*. Volume 1. Cambridge: Cambridge University Press, 1985

Tooley, Michael. *Abortion and Infanticide*. Oxford University Press: 1983.

Thomson, Judith Jarvis. *Rights, Restitution & Risk*. Cambridge: Harvard University Press, 1986.

Whitehead, Alfred North. *Process and Reality*. New York: Free Press, 1979.

Index

Index